dreams & relationships

dreams & relationships

Interpret Your Dreams,

Understand Your Emotions,

and Find Fulfillment

Nicholas Heyneman

CHRONICLE BOOKS

SAN FRANCISCO

Dreams & Relationships
Nicholas Heyneman

First published in the United States in 2000 by Chronicle Books LLC.

Conceived, created, and designed by
Duncan Baird Publishers Ltd.
Sixth Floor, Castle House
75-76 Wells Street
London W1P 3RE

Typeset in Mrs Eaves
Printed in China

Library of Congress Cataloging-in-Publication Data:
Heyneman, Nicholas E.
Dreams & relationships : interpret your dreams, understand your emotions, and find fulfillment/
written by Nicholas Heyneman.
p. cm.
ISBN 0-8118-2527-2
1. Dreams. 2. Interpersonal relations. I. Title. II. Title:
Dreams and relationships.
BF1099.I58H49 2000
154.6'3–dc21 99-14819
CIP

Commissioned artwork: Heidi Younger and Sandie Turchyn
Cover design: Sing Lin
Cover illustration: Heidi Younger

Distributed in Canada by
Raincoast Books
9050 Shaughnessy Street
Vancouver, B.C. V6P 6E5

7 9 10 8

Chronicle Books LLC
85 Second Street
San Francisco, CA 94105

www.chroniclebooks.com

PUBLISHERS' NOTES
To avoid the cumbersome repetition of "he or she" and "his or her", this
book breaks from traditional grammatical convention in using "they" or
"their" when referring to, for example, "a partner" or "a friend."

The Virtual Dream Kit was devised by DBP with guidance from Dr. Nicholas Heyneman.
Readers who have any comments about their experience of using the kit, or any suggestions
to make, are invited to write to or e-mail Dr. Heyneman (details on page 144).

To my parents, for getting it right.

CONTENTS

Introduction

*D*reams and Relationships brings a new approach to an aspect of our lives that everyone would agree is crucial to personal fulfillment. It ventures beyond conventional methods that view our interactions from the perspective of waking consciousness, to discover, through dreamwork, our emotional, intuitive and primal side, which is governed by the unconscious.

This book is relevant to all kinds of relationships — with lovers, family, friends, colleagues, and even enemies. It can be used alone, or with a partner or friend. It shows us how dreams can guide us to develop loving relationships and examines how they make sense of what seems inexplicable to our waking consciousness.

Through exercises and examples, we explore some highly original ways to communicate with a partner — including sharing dreams, creating telepathic dream links, and stimulating dreams to solve problems and answer questions. We examine the meaning of sexual dreams and introduce some playful yet powerful ways to bring intimacy alive. There is also a section on working with "virtual dreams" to bridge conflict and promote healing.

It is my sincere hope that this book will help you to discover what is most emotionally satisfying in every relationship and show you how vital are the people around you for happiness and emotional growth. Enjoy the journey.

Nick Heyneman

Dream Light

Dreams can be a wonderful source of self-understanding and personal insight. And relationship dreams have their own agenda of enlightenment. By giving us a clear view into the heart of a relationship, dreams disclose our true feelings, hopes, and desires, uninterrupted by the strictures of the waking mental censor. And they allow us to see others as they really are, not as we wish them to be. As a result, we are empowered to make better decisions about how to interact with our partners, friends, and family, and how to face and conquer the difficulties in any relationship, by dismantling resentments, and easing communication beyond the language of everyday life.

Extraordinary as all this may sound, the magic is really quite straightforward. To the waking eye, dreams often seem mysterious; but this is only because their logic differs radically from that of conscious thought. In this chapter we learn how to interpret the language of dreams and how to begin using it to strengthen all our relationships.

Introducing the Dream World

Through the ages, philosophers and scientists alike have debated the nature of dreaming. Why do we experience these mysterious nighttime dramas, and what secrets do they hold? Do dreams faithfully represent our waking lives or are they merely the background noise of the sleeping brain? As in every debate, there are extreme positions. Some scientists have asserted that dreams are merely the result of random electrical activity in the brain, produced in a deep stage of sleep, and any meaning we may infer from them is purely coincidental. Yet many philosophers (and some scientists, for that matter) have believed that dreams can be a source of profound truths, prophecies, and even supernatural powers. Not surprisingly, most psychologists fall somewhere between these two poles, proposing that dreams cannot extend our natural human faculties, although they can shed light on important aspects of our innermost feelings. But how do we learn to see by this light?

Although we also dream during other phases of sleep, our most vivid dreams occur within a state of consciousness known as Rapid Eye Movement (REM) sleep, so called because our eyes dart back and forth beneath our eyelids during this state. When we are in REM sleep, the brain pulsates in a particular fashion. While it is every bit as active as when we are awake, it possesses a unique signature — one whereby its most primitive parts (believed to control our basic functions such as breathing, and our emotions) dance in perfect rhythm with the much more recently evolved cerebral cortex (the "grey matter" that enables us to process information intelligently). What this means is that daytime logic is shut down

and replaced by "illogic:" for example, people sprout wings and fly; inanimate objects walk and talk; friends, family, and lovers appear and disappear in bodies that are not their own. This *dream logic* is as much at home in our sleep as rationality is in waking minds — and each is meaningless in the context of the other.

This is why, in order to make sense of our dreams, we should not take too literally the images that flit in front of our eyes. Instead, we should focus more on how we *feel* about what we see. Our dream emotions are likely to be more in tune with the reality of our waking emotions than many of the visual aspects of our dreams. To bring coherence to our mental chatter, we first need to search out each dream's emotional epicenter and look past its imagery to a place that our hearts know to be the truth. Once we have become practiced at taking emotional temperatures in

this way, we can go to the next stage of dream interpretation — the analysis of dream symbols and events as manifestations of the unconscious mind.

Dreams and Gender

No matter how much progress men and women make in sharing the same professions and undertaking the same roles within the family, there are fundamental distinctions between us. While we work toward equality in many parts of our lives, the success of our relationships, especially those across the sexes, depends on our understanding and appreciating differences between the genders. Somewhere along the line, merging gender roles in our society has become confused with merging gender characteristics. This psychological androgyny leads only to confusion: a man and a woman might reach the same conclusion on a given matter (or they might not!), but our thought processes and the way we communicate differ across the gender divide. If dreams are to help us improve our relationships, it is useful for us to understand gender-specific differences so that we can interpret the language of our unconscious more effectively.

As clichéd as it sounds, studies have proven that men have a tendency to speak and hear a language of status and position, while women tend to communicate more intimately and offer mutual support. Thus, telling a man what to do, however well-intentioned, is often interpreted as a put-down. Similarly, a woman may turn to a man to discuss a problem in the hope that he will offer her sympathy and understanding — but he will probably interpret her openness as a request for a solution, and instead of sympathy he will offer practical advice. Neither method is wrong — they are just alternative perspectives.

Bear in mind that men and women *are* very different, and that this is something to respect and cherish. Try to check yourself each time you give a gender response.

Consider the *animus* and *anima* – two dream archetypes (see pp.16–18) representing male and female. The animus, the male aspect, lies within the female consciousness; the anima, the female aspect, within the male. Each motivates us to empathize with someone of the opposite sex – perhaps a lover, parent, or sibling.

If you find it difficult to empathize in this way, try using your dreams to help. Before you go to bed, visualize your anima (if you are a man) or animus (if you are a woman) in any form you like: perhaps it is the blue center of a yellow flower, or a single water-lily in a still pond. Imagine the anima (or animus) growing larger until it represents half of the image you see (the blue center makes up half the flower, and the lily covers half the surface of the pond). Try to hold this image in your mind as you drift off to sleep and let your dreams be your teacher.

The Language of the Unconscious

While emotions form the nucleus of a dream, symbols add substance. Dream symbols are the unique language of the unconscious mind – a language that differs dramatically from the way in which images are consciously summoned by the waking mind, under the watchful eye of reason. The pioneer of psychoanalysis, Sigmund Freud (1856–1939), likened human consciousness to an iceberg floating in the ocean: the relatively small projection above the waterline represents waking reality (consciousness), while the massive body of the iceberg lying below the surface is our mysterious and complex unconscious. Before we begin to use dreams to help us enhance our relationships, we need to understand what might lie beneath the surface of the ocean of consciousness, and how that understanding can help. Freud's contemporary (and rival) Carl Jung (1875–1961) divided this vast expanse of the unconscious into two components: the *personal unconscious* and the *collective unconscious*.

Jung believed that the collective unconscious houses the emotional, intellectual, and spiritual experiences of every human being who has lived before us. It is the part of our mind that we all have in common, made up of the instincts, fears, appetites, myths, and symbols woven into the very fabric of the common ancestral mind. He believed that the collective unconscious extends the reach of our awareness and connects us to one another at the deepest level.

Jung gave the term *archetypes* to the symbols, laden with universal meaning, that reside in the collective unconscious. Examples include the animus and anima (see p.15), the elements of ourselves that show characteristics of the opposite sex. The

Listening to Your Inner Voice

Do dreams always offer us profound insights about ourselves? Does every dream fragment that we snatch and bring to the light of day truly reflect some aspect of waking life to which we would be wise to pay attention?

Most dreamworkers believe that, while the lion's share of dreams are meaningful and potentially illuminating, some are of little significance. If anything, we tend to over-interpret our dreams, reading meanings into every mysterious or intriguing feature. Perhaps certain dreams should be accepted merely as bizarre entertainments?

But if some dreams are meaningful and others are not, how do we tell the difference? The answer lies in the feelings that a dream embodies. Complex imagery, vivid symbol-ism, and an intricate plot mean little if the dream feels emotionally flat. Such dreams can often be dismissed as mental "static" – the mind's way of decoding the day and allowing itself to relax into sleep.

A dream with a significant message from the unconscious (for example, expressing an unac-knowledged tension within a relationship) will always feel special, and will have a distinct mood or emotional coloring, even if the images are vague or muddled. Dreams that well up from our innermost concerns always press for our attention – we will know them when they occur. Below is a list of dream characteristics that should make us take special note.

- *Any dream that embodies powerful emotions.*
- *Any dream that feels unique or out of the ordinary.*
- *Dream feelings that linger well into the day.*
- *Dream impressions or images that cannot be shaken from our minds.*
- *Dreams that include archetypal symbols.*
- *A recurring dream or dream emotion.*
- *A recurring theme regardless of imagery and symbolism.*

Shadow is the dark side of the ego, which we prefer to keep hidden; the Persona, the mask that we display to the outside world. The other main archetypes are the Divine Child (purity, innocence), the Wise Old Man or Woman (wisdom, knowledge), the Hero (inner growth), the Trickster (a complex figure who combines mischief with the corrective power of instinct) and the Great Mother (fertility, nurture, protection). Archetypes often appear in disguise: for example, the Persona might appear as a hobo or scarecrow; the Wise Old Man or Woman as a former teacher, and so on.

Although these are Jung's specific archetypes, it is possible to extend the list of universal symbols to include other images that evoke associations in all of us. For example, fire and snake have universal connotations: fire is passion, warmth, survival, but with potential for destruction or hurt (the connections with relationships are obvious); while the snake suggests venom, loss of innocence (the biblical tempter), and, according to the Freudian view, the penis. Images such as falling, flying, clothes, and nudity also tend to hold universal meaning.

The personal unconscious, on the other hand, is the vast reservoir of emotions, knowledge, attitudes, and beliefs that we accumulate through personal experience. Although genetic factors may play a part, the personal unconscious is largely formed by a lifetime of interactions — the essence of each and every past experience is distilled and assimilated into the unconscious mind, gelling and shaping what we call our personality. And, of course, our personality has far-reaching consequences for our relationships.

Ultimately, symbolism in dreams is mainly personal. When the appearance of something or someone seems inexplicable, we must judge its possible meanings in light of our own experience.

EXERCISE 1

Lifting the Lid on Interpretation

Dream interpretation is far more an art than a science. There are countless approaches, all of which have merit but none of which are perfect for everyone: the ultimate decision on the meaning of a dream must be made by the dreamer in the light of their own life and circumstances. You may find the following method — best tried with a partner — useful.

1. Visualize your dream — try to recapture as many images as you can. What do you feel? Remember that your emotions are the most important aspects. If the dream was long and complex, break it into smaller components to allow yourself to take a closer look at its emotions and symbolism.

2. Using your heart instead of your head, choose your primary aspect — the one symbol that somehow stands out from the rest.

3. Recount your dream to your partner as if you had only just met and they knew nothing about the images and emotions you describe. This will help you to focus on every detail.

4. Once you have recounted the dream, return to your primary aspect. What associations does the symbol have for you? What other possible overtones could it have?

5. Begin to sketch out a possible interpretation, bearing in mind the particular combination of emotion and symbolism. Try not to worry if you cannot reproduce a continuous logic — perhaps any gaps will be filled in by a later dream.

Remembering Dreams Together

Dreams often seem elusive — compelling dramas that quickly fade as our minds shift from sleep to waking consciousness. But it is not that the dreams themselves are mercurial, rather that our ability to recall them is underdeveloped. In the West we tend not to remember dreams because our culture invests little significance in doing so. In some other parts of the world, dreams are regarded as the storehouse of wisdom. Where dreams are highly prized, virtually everyone is urged to recollect them. Hunters in many Native North American tribes traditionally used dreams to guide them to the best hunting grounds, and today the tribespeople of Gabon, in Central Africa, judge the guilt or innocence of someone charged with a crime according to the content of the elders' dream revelations. People who bear such responsibilities have acquired carefully honed powers of dream recall.

The resounding message, therefore, is that if we consider dreamwork worthy of our time and effort, we too will begin to develop an ability to remember our dreams more clearly — especially if someone we trust is able to help us. Just like physical exercise, dream recall is easier and more enjoyable with the support of another person, who can urge us to keep going when we feel like giving up, and challenge us to try harder when we become complacent. The mutual encouragement, enthusiasm, and interest generated from working with a partner greatly enhance our ability to master dreamwork, and remembering our dreams together makes dream recall much easier than it would be if we tried to do it alone.

The Trigger–Recall Challenge

Tests have proven that certain stimuli will trigger particular dreams. Using this principle, you can test your partner's powers of dream recall with a playful experiment. Your partner should lie in bed as if they were going to sleep, and close their eyes. Then, once they are feeling comfortable and relaxed, gently apply one of the following stimuli to trigger their dreams.

- *A gentle spray of water on the skin to inspire dreams of feeling wet, such as swimming or being caught in the rain.*
- *A soft caress of the dreamer's toes, neck, or abdomen with the fingertips or a feather to induce sensual or even erotic dreams.*
- *A scent or smell, such as a particular perfume or aftershave, wafted beneath the dreamer's nose, to trigger dreams that include a memory or person associated with that scent.*

When you both wake up in the morning, prompt your partner's recall of the previous night's dreams by applying the same stimulus to them again.

As you do so, the memory of the dream may come back, enabling them to give a full and vivid account. You can gently encourage this process of recollection by softly speaking words associated with the particular dream stimulus, as you reapply it. Use the following words as a starting point, adding others that you think may aid your partner's recall.

- *If your stimulus was the water, repeat coaxingly these words: trickle, lap, pitter-patter, splash.*
- *If you chose to stroke your partner gently, say these words: caress, softness, embrace, passion, love, tenderness.*
- *If your stimulus was a scent, repeat words linked to the scent: your own name if it was your perfume or aftershave; the name of the place from where you yourself remember it; and so on.*

Sometimes the conscious mind seems to block the transfer of dream images from the world of sleep into waking reality. This may mean that the mind's defense mechanism has been activated to prevent the dreams from revealing or provoking painful feelings — especially those that we suppress during waking hours. Concentrate on tuning into your unconscious, and capturing fleeting images on paper, the moment you wake up. It helps, of course, to keep a notebook and pen or pencil by your bed.

It is crucial to make your record first thing in the morning, since even the most committed dreamworker will forget a night's dreams over the course of a busy day. With a partner, you might try setting your alarm clock five minutes earlier, spending the time you have gained talking through each other's dreams to fix the dream images in your minds while they are still fresh. If you

find that you remember your dreams particularly well one morning, try to analyze why. Perhaps you unwittingly created an environment more conducive to dream recall by, for example, changing the temperature of your bedroom or varying your nighttime routine.

Remembering a dream is not like remembering a real event. Instead of concentrating all your powers of reason, the secret is to relax those powers and let the details float to the surface of your mind, taking care not to censor any aspects that you might find uncomfortable.

If you are enthusiastic about remembering your dreams, your powers of recall, like any art, will improve with practice. Try to build up a momentum of remembering, each day attempting to recapture a little more detail about the previous night's dream, and you will begin to notice some improvement. A good night's sleep is preferable, as dream recall seems harder when we are tired.

EXERCISE 2

Letting in the Light of Recall

There is nothing inherently difficult about learning to remember dreams: we simply have to open our minds to the value of dreams and give them "permission" to come to the surface, which requires us to suspend the controlling powers of reason. It helps to work on dream recall with your partner.

1. Sit down with your partner and talk about your desire to remember your dreams. Discuss what it means to each of you and what you both hope to accomplish.

2. Generate a simple affirmation to stimulate vivid dreams — for example, "We are open to our dreams." The wording is unimportant — find an affirmation with which you both feel comfortable. At bedtime, whisper the affirmation out loud as you drift off to sleep.

3. When you wake up the following morning, lie still, keeping yourself in a half-waking, half-sleeping state, and let your mind wander. Be alert to any images, impressions, or feelings that come to you. Keep a dream journal and record these impressions as soon as you are completely awake.

4. Discuss your dreams with your partner — the sooner after waking the better, but ideally when you are both able to give the talk your full attention. Make your descriptions as vivid as possible, capturing the mood as well as the imagery and narrative. Ask each other lots of open questions to spark off new thoughts, offering each other plenty of encouragement.

The Emotions of Sleep

Dream life is a netherworld of swirling emotions: raw, undisguised, and free from the shackles of unconscious repression and the need to conform to the social laws of waking reality. The core meaning of a dream is how it feels: the emotions coalesce to form its very essence, which is often a far more reliable guide to the dream's meaning than the visual images that tend normally to catch our attention.

While waking emotions can sometimes be misleading, we can rely upon dreams to display truthfully the entire spectrum of feelings intrinsic to relationships — whether positive emotions such as joy and excitement, or darker feelings such as sadness, anger, and frustration. In turn, dreams can help us come to terms with our waking emotions: they can guide us in dealing with disabling guilt, or teach us how to infuse new life into a relationship when it is most needed.

In this chapter we explore how to recognize and utilize dream feelings, and what they mean to us in the context of our relationships, past and present.

Volcanoes and Moonquakes

Dreams erupt with emotions. Some smother us with the violent force of a volcano, while others provide a gentle nudge — the slight tremor of a moonquake. Waking consciousness is vigilantly protected from emotional assaults too intense to withstand, as we automatically erect psychological barriers that let in only those feelings we can manage. Dream emotions have no such defensive barriers. They are honest, straightforward, and lay bare feelings that in waking life stay buried beneath the business of each day or are misinterpreted when we subject them to rational analysis. The lingering nature of dream emotions (for example, the feelings of dream sadness that we carry into morning wakefulness) is evidence enough that we should take notice of them.

Draw a circle on a large sheet of paper and write around the inside circumference all the words that you might use to describe the dream emotions you remember experiencing. Place comparable emotions together — for example, jealousy, envy, and resentment, or rapture, joy, and euphoria. Work with a thesaurus, which will give you lists of words arranged according to proximity of meaning. On the outside of the circle note down colors that seem appropriate to the emotions you have written, and any images you come across in dreams that regularly tend to be saturated in these feelings. This emotional circle of dreams has two purposes. You can use it to build up a map of the emotional

content of your dream life, by adding images and narratives around the outer edge as they occur in your dreams; and you can also use it as a quick-reference tool to find the words to help you identify a particular emotion.

Locating words for emotions is important, because it enables you to communicate your dreams accurately to your partner or a friend, as well as to make precise entries in your dream diary. Bear in mind, however, that sometimes you will have to move away from the conventional vocabulary of the emotional spectrum. For example, there is no accepted emotional noun or adjective for feeling hollow or empty inside, or for feeling that something important has been stolen from you. So express your feelings by drawing simple pictures instead. If your dreams offer you comparable images (an empty box, a burglary), any previous work you have done to translate your emotions into visual terms may help you enormously in the process of interpretation. As we begin to probe our dream feelings, greater emotional breadth and depth will emerge in our dreaming lives.

Pushing Back the Walls

The psychologist Erik Erikson once described intimacy as finding yet losing oneself in another. In the most successful kinds of relationship, we discover new and wonderful things about ourselves, setting free the unabridged version of who we are, while at the same time becoming enriched by our intimacy with another which constantly gives us fresh perspectives on life. This deceptively simple goal can seem all too elusive. One common experience that can prevent us from reaching Erikson's Grail is the feeling, at some point in the relationship, that it is becoming claustrophobic – as though the walls of intimacy are bearing down on us and preventing us from moving freely as individuals.

Most teenagers go through a stage of feeling trapped in a family, unable to reach personal fulfillment because their freedom seems compromised by their parents, and sometimes also by siblings with whom they share their home. Many, on reaching adulthood, cherish their individuality so much that they have difficulty adjusting to a mature relationship.

In dreams, such emotions often present themselves in terms of entrapment and enclosure: walls may close in on us, or we may be underwater and unable to break through to the surface. We may even find that, in a dream, our own identity has merged with that of our partner – when we look in a mirror, the face that we see has their features, not our own. When we wake up from such a dream, we may feel tense and short of breath, as if we are suffocating. This is because our unconscious mind is asking us to take stock of our emotions and deal with them, as indeed we must if we wish to put our relationship on a healthier footing.

Relationship claustrophobia, though powerfully felt, is often more imagined than real, and we can sometimes conquer it by a mere adjustment of perspective. Spend time thinking about your partner as a liberator: what freedoms or privileges have they given you? Translate these gifts into visual terms, remembered or imaginary (views of distant horizons, clouds in an endless sky, two waterbirds on a vast lake, and so on), and hold such images in your mind before you go to sleep, in the hope that they will counteract your dreams of entrapment.

Scan your dreams also for signs of any unresolved issues that may explain your feelings of claustrophobia more specifically. Talk through your dream life with your partner and use dialogue techniques (see pp.76–9) to isolate and tackle any deep-seated problems.

Emotional Needs

It is part of the human condition to be needy from time to time. Most of us feel dependent upon other people for emotional nourishment: we may crave the warmth, closeness, understanding, and companionship that only someone else can provide. When we are without a significant relationship, our energies, consciously or not, often focus on searching for one. Even if we are happily involved, or have a strong network of supportive friends, the fluctuations in our confidence and sense of security can sometimes generate an emotional craving.

In waking life our needs, even when they are strong, are not always recognizable to ourselves: they can be obscured by the psychological defenses we erect. We may experience a vague sense of dissatisfaction or of emptiness, but nothing more concrete. Feelings like these should be taken as a cue for us to listen to the messages of our dream life, which is usually able to throw light on our inner yearnings and crystallize general unease into a set of more particular emotional needs.

Dreams work in terms of either positive or negative imagery: the only way to distinguish one from the other is to pay attention to the emotions they bring forth. For example, a dream of love-making filled with longing may indicate a need for a more satisfying sex life; whereas an intercourse dream linked with slight feelings of nausea could suggest that your partner is making excessive physical demands on you, or that sex feels wrong because there is some difficulty that needs to be addressed. By attuning ourselves to the moods and feelings of our dreams we can articulate our waking emotions more constructively — for our own benefit, for that of our partner, and for the sake of the relationship.

Voices from the Past

Sometimes the emotions of a dream are clear, but their source remains hidden. This is because dreams are often anachronistic. In other words, dreams of feeling starved of love might not be directly related to our partner, but instead might be a throwback to lovelessness in an earlier relationship, or even in childhood. However much love our current partner gives us, it will never be enough to assuage this historic thirst.

If emotions such as emptiness are rooted in the past, your dreams will give you hints. If your partner appears wearing unusual clothes, could they belong to a relative or a former lover? Obsolete settings, such as steam engines or music from a different era, can also help you to recognize a "transference" dream of this type. You may find, moreover, that your dream images look larger than life, as if viewed from the perspective of a child.

It is a mistake to think of emotional needs as being essentially similar to basic physical needs such as warmth, food, and sleep: we cannot expect them to be satisfied so promptly. We must accept that if our partner is not answering our needs, a fundamental shift of attitude might be needed within the relationship, and that this will make demands on the time and patience of each one of us. Use the imagery of your dreams to explain the lack that you feel, and do some of the dreamwork exercises in this book to work patiently toward a resolution. Look out for, and make a note of, any positive imagery or emotions that dreams offer during this period — these can serve as reminders of how precious your relationship is to you. If both of you cherish this value, take heart from your common purpose. Work together on your dreams to improve your mutual empathy and move toward fulfillment.

Panic and Calm

Even within people who are emotionally resilient by character there lies a panic alarm, which occasionally registers feelings of fear, loss, bewilderment, abandonment, and other negative states. In relationships we tend to panic when we fear that we are about to lose what is precious to us. We might feel this after a heated argument, or when our partner describes in glowing terms someone whom we begin to perceive as a rival. But sometimes we panic only in our dreams, because in waking life we have not come to understand the real risk of loss that accompanies certain tendencies current in our relationship.

Let us say that one night you dream of being thrown into a dungeon and left without food or water, and that the following week you have a dream in which you are flying in a two-seated plane as a navigator — but you suddenly discover that the pilot's seat is empty. Each dream is saturated in feelings of panic. Your inner voice is telling you that it is time to take stock, to rebuild communication bridges that you have allowed to fall into disrepair. You may eventually discover that the panic is related to a professional situation, a friendship, or a family matter rather than to your relationship with your partner. But why not start with the relationship and make a conscious effort to open up an imaginative and creative dialogue with your lover? Describe the dream and find out what insights they have to offer. Such dreamwork may lead inward (into the relationship) or outward (to the workplace, friendship, or family situation), but whatever turns out to be the root cause of your dreams of panic, the dialogue can only be constructive.

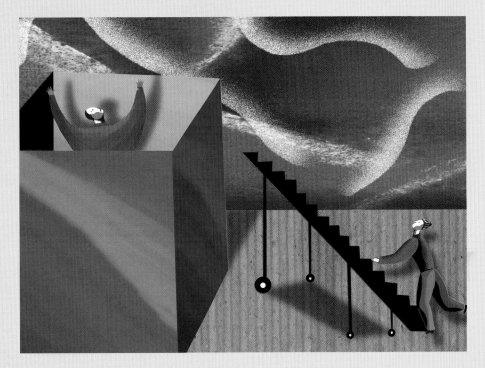

Images of calm can be consciously used as a corrective to panic. If your dreams of panic feature falling from a height, you might decide with your partner to spend a vacation on a plain or prairie to provide an imaginative antidote that might enter your dreams. Another approach would be to defuse the panic image by generating positive feelings around the same circumstances – for example, by taking a ride in a cablecar, or a sight-seeing trip by helicopter. You will still need to address the emotions that gave rise to the panic in the first place, but at least your dreams may become less troubled.

If a dream of calm occurs one night to break a series of panic dreams, hold on to it as a beacon of hope. Your anxieties are probably temporary. By working through them with your partner it should be possible to reach the tranquillity that has been promised by such a heartening vision.

Joy and Sadness

Opposite poles of an emotional spectrum, joy and sadness are abundantly expressed in dreams. Sometimes they reflect the events that are currently happening in our waking life — for example, a dream of joy could represent our own or our partner's promotion, or sadness at the loss of a cherished object such as an engagement ring. But sometimes dreams of joy and sadness can occur as a result of the need to release hitherto repressed feelings from the past.

In the range between these two extremes are many shades of feeling that are less dramatic and therefore unobtrusive, so that we do not always notice them in our dreams. For example, a dream of a still, natural landscape is likely to reflect a quiet contentment with our waking life rather than emotional emptiness (unless, of course, the mood of the dream indicates otherwise). Learn from your dreams themselves how to express these intermediate states to your partner — perhaps through an image conceived by your dream. Get into the habit of describing how you feel, even if this involves pinning down a nuance that you have never articulated before.

When interpreting the mood of our dreams, we should always be careful not to misunderstand a wistfulness that is not sadness in the usual sense, but regret that the wonders of the dream world are over, leaving us with mundane reality once more. Wistfulness surrounds many of the mysteries of dreaming, precisely because they are mysteries. If on waking we experience a sense of frustration, it could simply be that part of us yearns to stay in the dream world — or, more mundanely, longs to be able to fall asleep again instead of facing the day's challenges.

The Surprise of Opposites

Usually, we find it easy to relate the dream emotions of joy and sadness to the circumstances of our waking lives, but there are times when the dream mood is unexpected: euphoria in times of emotional difficulty, a chord of melancholy sounded when our waking music seems pitched to a key of contentment.

Sometimes happy dreams at a time of waking sorrow can be regarded as dreams of compensation — an attempt by our unconscious to bolster our strength in the face of adversity. But perhaps the best way to interpret such surprises is as threads of our history's tapestry: leftover feelings from times when our emotional landscape looked very different. Conversely, if the thread is joyous, we should take this as a sign of hope. However great our difficulties seem, there is no reason why we cannot recapture such happiness in the future.

Think of sadness in dreams as something that absolves us from being sad in reality — on waking we can feel that we have done our sorrowing already, during the night, when we were exempt from a more constructive approach to our difficulties. Let this be enough to make us feel that we have given adequate expression to our despondency. If the problems stem from a relationship, it is better to face up to them and tackle the issues constructively and cooperatively with our partner, than to dwell on negative emotions.

Joy in dreams is a great blessing — whether it reflects true happiness in a relationship or merely reminds us of the potential for happiness. Tell your partner about such uplifting feelings and establish them as the keynote of your relationship, even when more melancholic notes temporarily drown the melody of ecstasy.

Lost in the Snow
Case Study

Unexpected prompts in waking life can bring clarity to the meaning of a recent dream. In this case study, an ornament that had gone unnoticed for many years became a vital reminder of the emotional warnings in the previous night's dream.

Paul never paid much attention to his dreams until he and his wife Christine began to drift apart after seventeen years of marriage. Their problems built up so gradually that they were hardly noticeable. There were no real fights: superficially they still seemed to get along well, even when handling minor crises together, but the passion that once kept their relationship buoyant was slowly being snuffed out. Intimacy and sex became almost non-existent. When Paul was promoted at work, he celebrated with friends, and Christine did not learn of his promotion until two weeks later.

Christine began feeling increasingly empty. It was as if she and her husband were no longer the friends and lovers they had once been, but merely two people keeping house together. She tried to discuss her feelings with Paul, and her parents, but was always rebuffed. No one understood her growing discontent because, from the outside, their marriage seemed solid. She was told that no marriage is perfect and that she ought to be thankful for what she had. For his part, Paul thought that she was overreacting and refused to take her seriously, especially when she asked if he was having an affair. With nowhere to turn, Christine felt as if her spirit were slowly being drained of its life.

Then Paul had a very important dream. He saw Christine leaving home by herself to go hiking into the mountains in the middle of winter. Although he thought it curious that she would go alone and in such cold conditions, he did not pay too much attention. Then what seemed like weeks or maybe even months passed and she never returned home. He mentioned the trip to her family but they also seemed unconcerned. He was considering going off to look for Christine, but he was too busy, so he brushed aside the idea that she might be in danger. Then Paul had a dream within his dream: he saw his wife lying still and silent, face down in the snow, growing blue with cold. He knew that if he did not immediately rescue her, she would die. He awoke in a panic.

Paul did not immediately understand his dream. But its feelings flooded back when he caught sight of a "snowstorm" souvenir from a vacation they had taken in Paris — a model of the Eiffel Tower in a plastic bubble that you shake to stir up an imitation blizzard. This made him deeply nostalgic and suddenly the meaning of the dream dawned on him. Overwhelmed by the intensity of his feelings, Paul related his dream, and the insight it had given him, to Christine. As a result, the couple decided to attend counseling sessions together to help them rebuild the loving relationship they had once shared.

Mirrors of Guilt

Guilt is the most misunderstood emotion of all. Sometimes it is the useful prompting of the conscience, telling us that our thoughts or actions are wrong — and will lead us into trouble. But sometimes guilt stems from external rather than internal pressures, such as a friend repeatedly trying to persuade you to do something against your will.

Take three examples. André felt bad because he knew in his heart that he was putting his career before time spent with his wife and children. Antonia felt uncomfortable because she was 15 years older than her new lover, and she was conscious of people staring at them. Andrew was anxious because his parents were dropping hints that they wanted him to lend money to his impoverished brother, even though the brothers hardly ever saw each other. These are three different types of guilt: the inward (conscience), the programmatic (social conditioning), and the relational (emotional blackmail).

All three types of guilt are likely to appear in dreams, in different manifestations, but each has a mood that is usually unmistakable. André dreamed that his wife and children were being attacked by an intruder while he watched helplessly through an impenetrable plate-glass window. Antonia dreamed of standing naked in a line of well-dressed people outside a concert hall. Andrew dreamed that the dog he had as a childhood pet was caught in a hunter's trap.

These examples characterize the different categories of guilt dreams. Inward and relational guilt dreams tend to focus on the person (or people) whom we believe, in our hearts, we are harming in some way — which need not,

of course, be someone else, for we might just as easily believe deep down that we are harming ourselves. Programmatic guilt dreams tend to focus on ourselves, and often display an element of shame (guilt made public).

While dreams of guilt can be useful if they tell us when we need to right a wrong, external forms of guilt can be dangerous because they can give us erroneous signposts. Sometimes the pressure of other people's opinions is so strong that the inward wish to assert our own personal, intuitive conscience collapses under the strain. Dreams of shame at our own nakedness, in particular, tend to indicate influences that perhaps we should summon up the strength to resist — while at the same time asking ourselves whether the independent line we are taking is worth the social price we shall have to pay.

Passion and Love

Passion burns at the core of the libido, which according to Freud is the source of all human energy. It ignites and inspires us, and both drains and rejuvenates us. It is the soul of art, and the fire of love. It is passion that gives a relationship its depth and intensity, and it appears in dreams in many guises.

When we think of passion, erotic dreams naturally come to mind. Many of these are playful and exciting, and can arouse waking sensuality, but others may leave the dreamer in turmoil, or feeling embarrassed, even ashamed. Erotic dreams rarely mean what the imagery at first seems to portray, so they should always be interpreted with care (see pp.58–61).

The mood of passion can be described as an emotional enlargement that fills the body, mind, and heart with a mixture of desire and the potential for fulfilling that desire (lust satisfies only the body and the mind). Passion is often at its most intense just prior to achieving its object, for once the one whom we adore reciprocates with equal ardor, it is not unusual for our passion to wane. This emotional paradox can be reflected in our dreams when, for example, intimacy with our lover has a curious detachment — that vital spark of passion is missing.

Dreams will often pick up on the romantic vocabulary of flowers, scent, luxurious draperies, billowing bedclothes, low-key lighting, and so on. Touch plays a large part in passionate dreams. Commonly they also draw upon the most profound stories that have played such a prominent part in Western culture — for example, Romeo and Juliet, Tristan and Isolde, Hero and Leander.

If we dream of sex and death in close proximity, this is possibly an influence from myth and literature (and, these days, the movies), although we have to ask why this theme became popular in the first place. The answer may be that passion, like death, involves surrender. Dreams of death should not be regarded as morbid, but should be taken as a reflection of intense feelings.

A question commonly asked is, "Can dreams tell us when we are in love?" One positive sign is dreaming of the loved one as an idealized or inaccessible figure — for example, a statue, a king or queen, or an angel or other celestial being. However, love, being a turbulent state, can also bring about nightmares, especially ones associated with the fear of loss. On the other hand, a lover's feelings are some-times rewarded with radiantly transcendental dreams, which make us feel on waking, if only for a moment, that we have glimpsed a heavenly realm.

Emotional Surges

During trying times, dreams can help us to deal with our powerful emotions and equip us with the emotional strength and self-confidence to see a crisis through to its conclusion. Of course, they will also reflect our turbulent state of mind by generating negative images and moods – for example, if we are jealous, we might vividly imagine passionate acts of betrayal. However, there are several possible approaches that, combined in a conscious program of visualization and dream-work, will enable us to muster the inner resources to ride out the emotional storm.

When we are overcome by surges of emotion we tend to perform an act of emotional surrender, allowing them to take us over so that, in effect, those feelings are magnified. The problem lies in absorbing ourselves too much in our emotions. They are not our whole self, only part of it; and however strongly surges of emotion manifest themselves, whether in waking life or dreams, they can be tamed through a conscious act of control.

The first step is to make affirmations to this effect, especially just before you sleep, such as: "My true self is indestructible and limitless" or "I find strength and harmony in my emotions." Meditate on an image of the self before you sleep – perhaps as a bird, or a tree, or some other natural symbol. Remember also that your dreams, however accurately they reflect your concerns, can bring only messages to waking reality, not real experiences. If they speak to you of deep and disturbing emotions, this should not be taken as a bulletin saying that the battle for peace has been lost. On the contrary, you have in your possession a valuable map of the enemy lines – now go on to make the best use of it.

EXERCISE 3

Summoning a Dream Hero

A powerscript is a set of visual images that we consciously imagine in order to transform ourselves into beings of great strength and energy, able to overcome or deter even the most formidable obstacles. This is a way to gain mastery over our dreams and subdue some of their most disturbing features in a way that will spill over into waking life.

1. Choose an image of invincibility. You might imagine yourself wearing impenetrable body armor, or cloaked in a "superhero" cape that endows you with extraordinary strength. Or you might prefer to imagine that your partner or best friend has this magic device, and is at hand to protect you. Or then again you might like to imagine a stranger similarly equipped — a gallant knight of the imagination.

2. Before sleep, visualize your protector (or yourself) magically equipped. Feel the protective aura radiating from them (or you), enveloping you in a deep sense of security.

This figure will patrol your dreams, protecting your true self from any destructive forces unleashed by negative emotions.

3. When you wake up in the morning, think back over any dream you have had during the night. Even if your figure did not make a positive appearance, they were there in the background, preventing your dream emotions from infiltrating into waking consciousness. Any such feelings that occurred in your dream were there for instructive purposes only: your protector ensured that they were neutralized and unable to affect your waking mind.

The Dream Path of Love

At every stage of a relationship, from the nervous initial glance, through the magical first kiss and the playful beginnings, to the binding love that can weather life's storms, dreams faithfully support and guide our every step down the path of love.

As we progress in our relationship, our dreams appear especially vivid when issues of love, compatibility, independence, and commitment come into high relief and we are faced with dilemmas about how to proceed. By tuning into our dream life we can gain insights into whether or not we are on the right course, and with growing acquaintance we can learn how to love and be loved, how to share ourselves with another, and how to attain mutual harmony and fulfillment.

In this chapter we trace the stages of love from the first overtures to long-term commitment. We learn how dreams can clarify our feelings and sharpen our intuition so that we can make the healthiest relationship choices, and how dreams can aid communication with our partner at every crucial stage.

The Open Heart

For many of us, the search for a partner absorbs much of our energy and occupies our minds, whether consciously or unconsciously, from the moment we reach sexual maturity. This is our natural instinct, ensuring the survival of the species; yet it also reflects the deep-seated urge to make ourselves feel whole by finding the right person with whom to share our lives.

Some of us may feel that the key to wholeness is remaining single. But if we have a profound need for a relationship, dreams are not fooled by rationalizations and other psychological defenses that hinder us in our search — after all, they are in direct contact with our unconscious. If your dreams feature barren landscapes, or figures seeking comfort from one another, they probably indicate an unsatisfied craving for a love-bond. People who are single by choice may also, to their surprise, find feelings of loneliness or isolation in their dream life.

If you are looking for a partner, it helps to think of your dreams as allies in the quest — try putting questions to them before you drift off to sleep, in the form of imagined situations. For example, you might visualize yourself and a partner visiting their parents, which in turn prompts dreams that illuminate your anxieties about becoming enmeshed in another person's life. Or a dream might reveal some detail that later sparks off a coincidence in connection with someone you have met. Do not hesitate to follow up such coincidences if your heart tells you that they are a positive sign. If they encourage you to explore your options more energetically, such tentative pointers can be one of dreaming's most valuable gifts.

EXERCISE 4

Hues of Love

The following exercise translates the subtleties of your psychological needs into colors, which may give you clearer signposts in your quests for a suitable partner, as well as cues for you to use to prompt dream revelations. The colors and their meanings are as follows: blue is creative, emotional, cerebral, and remote; red is passionate, fiery, driven, and unpredictable; green is logical, compulsive, and jealous; gold is wise, determined, and uncompromising; orange is warm, courageous, and elusive; violet is intuitive, spiritual, and dreamy; brown is earthy, practical, and melancholic; black is mysterious, powerful, and alluring; white is virtuous, ethereal, and unsettled.

1. Consider which three colors characterize your personality, following the attributes of each color listed above. Then, based upon your chosen palette, consider which colors would best complement your own and supply the qualities that you lack — these represent your ideal partner.

2. Weave the colors of your potential partner into your dreams. Each night, before you fall asleep, set the scene by visualizing the place, figures, and objects you wish to appear. If, for example, you are seeking someone represented by blue, imagine symbols of sky or water; if you would prefer a person with green characteristics, imagine lush landscapes or gardens, and so on.

3. In waking life, look out for your chosen colors in potential partners. With practice, you will soon home in automatically on those who complement your own colors.

A Meeting of Souls

Have you ever wondered why you can be intensely attracted to someone you have just met whose appeal seems to go beyond the physical? Or why certain rare friendships feel so natural, comfortable, and inevitable? From antiquity, many people have sought wholeness in a love that integrates body and soul, and when we meet someone who seems to be in some way already our friend, so that communication is almost like self-communion, it is likely that we have found a soulmate — someone whose inner spirit seems perfectly to complement our own.

Many dreamworkers believe in the concept of past lives, and hold that we unconsciously surround ourselves with friends, lovers, and even enemies who have played a prominent role in a previous incarnation. Whether or not this concept strikes us as plausible will depend upon our religious and philosophical beliefs, but the notion that souls are intertwined for eternity enjoys a long tradition in both Eastern and Western mysticism.

Even if we feel that we have not yet met a soulmate in waking life, we can sometimes encounter them in the dream world. When this happens, you will have a very special dream: it will feel unique, as if it is somehow a glimpse of a different era, perhaps endowed with an almost prophetic quality, or perhaps resonant with an echo of the past.

When you are fortunate enough to have a soulmate as a partner, dreams can help you to understand and celebrate the unique closeness of your relationship. It would be a tremendous waste of potential not to explore dream dialogues together (see pp.76–9) and not to attempt dream sharing (see pp.88–9).

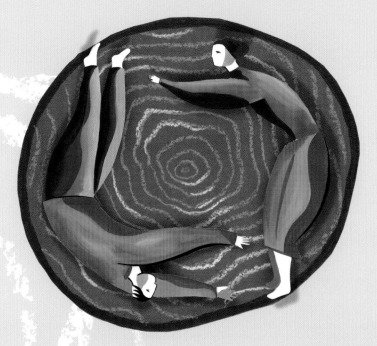

By piecing together your dreams with those of your partner like a jigsaw puzzle, and interchanging scenes, settings, and characters, you may well discover a combination that springs into sharp focus, loaded with significance for you both.

It can be intriguing to try to use your soulmate's dream life as an oracle to cast light on your own problems outside the relationship — in work situations, difficulties with parents or siblings, and so on. The theory behind this idea is that the soulmate, although deeply empathetic to your personal issues, is at the same time still detached enough from them to be able to generate clearer messages for you — after all, when reading a book or newspaper, it is better to hold the pages a couple of feet in front of you than to have your nose pressed up against the paper. Try prompting your soulmate to dream about your own concerns by quietly free-associating (see p.78 and p.79) around them before you drift off to sleep together — you can then compare results in the morning.

The Agony and the Ecstasy
Case Study

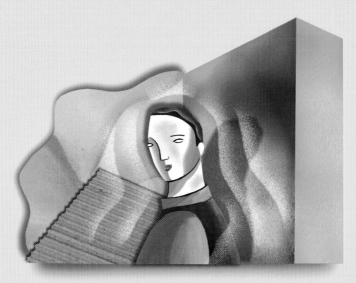

Jason and Tara had an extremely volatile relationship — but they were soulmates. This case study shows that once we have found our soulmate, we can usually use our deep link with each other to put our relationship back on course.

Jason and Tara could never just talk. Their interactions always burst with emotion, whether joy or anger. Whenever they tried to discuss something, their conversations became confrontational, as each battled ceaselessly for control over the other. And then, following every vicious fight, there was an equally intense reconciliation when their intimacy and feelings of connection knew no bounds.

In fact, the one area left unscathed by their arguments was their sex life — by far the best either had ever had.

Aware that their marriage was crumbling away, and tired of all the fighting, Jason and Tara decided to face up to their problems, and try to make the relationship work constructively — but they wanted to fix it without losing the passion that they had in bed.

The couple had heard that dream-work might help them to establish whether the love-hate relationship of waking life extended to their unconscious — were they, deep down, incompatible? They began by keeping separate dream journals. To neither's surprise, each reported a range of wildly vivid dreams: turbulent, emotionally charged, and often sexual. Excitingly, however, the couple found that they were dreaming in parallel. Dream frequency, intensity, and emotional and thematic content were all highly correlated. The parallels were too numerous to be merely coincidence — it became obvious that the couple were linked in a profound way.

They experimented to see if they could use this deep connection to their advantage. Jason and Tara began a mutual dream journal in which each would examine the other's dreams. When put together, their dreams revealed an endless struggle for control.

To try to break this pattern, the couple tried repeating affirmations each night to stimulate dreams of cooperation instead of aggression. Holding hands before they went to sleep, they spoke to each other of doves, tranquil waters, and gentle, cooling breezes. Gradually, their dreams progressed from bitter images of struggle and conquest to those of compromise and harmony, with symbols of mutual support: for example, Tara dreamed that the couple were rowing a boat together, their oar strokes perfectly synchronized, with the hull of the boat cutting seamlessly through the water.

As Jason and Tara's dreams became less aggressive, so too did their waking life. They learned to tame their competitiveness and to support each other. Moreover, they found that they still experienced all the intense physical passion that they had always had, but that it was now founded in deep love and respect.

Unfolding Attraction

When we are attracted to someone, our life suddenly seems vibrant with possibilities. Our imagination starts working wildly, and we read volumes of meaning into sometimes quite trivial signs. We start to daydream, and at the same time we lay down intricate plans to create situations that will further our cause. At night our minds are tossed by dreams that are often colorful and sensual, as well as full of frenetic movement, with a predilection for primal symbols such as fire, volcanoes, and high winds.

Once you have decided to pursue the object of your attraction, allow your dreams to guide you. Bear in mind that conscious planning alone will not bring you what you are looking for, because attraction is a mysterious chemistry, with its roots in the unconscious. Avoid taking your dreams too literally: principally, you are looking for clues about the nature of your attraction, the qualities in your potential partner to which you are especially drawn. For example, you might dream of the person crouching in a field and all the birds in the area flocking around their head. As always, the interpretation will depend on what you already know. You might feel that the dream image is consistent with signs of kindness in the person to whom you are attracted — the birds are trusting, and know they will be fed. The image makes you more attentive in waking life to this aspect of their character, and this in turn will strengthen your conviction that you are on the right path. However, if you feel the birds are enigmatic, perhaps their relevance is that they are hiding your potential partner's face, which suggests that further acquaintance is needed before you become too involved.

Secret Love

Occasionally, we will be attracted to someone whom we know deep down can never bring us happiness. It could be that their love is committed elsewhere, perhaps within a long-term relationship. It could be that the person has no feelings for us — and that we know this either from concrete words or gestures, or by instinct. Then again, there may be some other obstacle: a difference in social background, or a huge age gap, or a professional connection that intimacy could only damage. If we keep such an attraction secret, its clandestine nature only fuels our desire and makes us fantasize — especially in our dream lives. Alternatively, we may try to forget the attraction but, when we do, our dreams persist in offering us tantalizing reminders.

The question of what to do about an impossible attraction can be straightforward. It may feel like a difficult choice, but it is not — especially if the object of the attraction is in a committed relationship — we must simply stay away.

Much depends on how free we are (and how much hurt it would cause others) to follow our instincts. The message from dreams can take scant consideration of social realities — for example, if you have a family, passionate dreams about your next-door neighbor are best taken as a warning, not an encouragement. Remember that affairs are rarely successful for any of the parties involved. But if both you and your would-be partner are free, your dream passion can motivate you to overcome inhibitions and embark on an experimental adventure.

If you decide not to act, how can dreams help you to exorcize an attraction? One method is to disarm them, so that they no longer whisper passionate incitements into your sleeping mind. Try meditating before sleep on abstract patterns, or on non-specific objects for which you have strong feelings — for example, you might visualize the earth itself as a precious jewel suspended in space.

Early Days

Falling in love is an enthralling experience — we are swept away by a swirling mix of excitement, nervousness, and desire. But compatibility is the backbone of any successful relationship, and in the earliest weeks and months we are still uncertain whether the seeds of harmony are taking root. We may supress aspects of ourselves so as not to reveal our differences too starkly, or to seem to want too much too soon. The strength of our desires, combined with the element of concealment, makes our dreams especially vivid and deeply felt at this time.

Propelled by sexual desire and emotional need, dreams of a blossoming relationship tend to be several steps ahead of the reality, and we must resist the temptation to keep pace with their hectic impatience. Otherwise we race through the vital stages of mutual acquaintance, and risk building an edifice whose foundations have not been properly established. It is better to take hints from the scenarios, narratives, and symbolism of our dreams, and reflect privately on those hints, than to interpret their urgency literally. To dream of being on vacation together does not mean that now is the right time to propose such an undertaking.

Our dreams will not be able to provide foolproof answers to the question of compatibility, but they will almost certainly reveal the major issues you need to think about. Any conflicts or tensions in a dream specially associated with the object of your attraction, should alert you to the possibility that the prospects of mutual happiness may be remote. However, such tension may reflect perfectly natural and normal anxieties — the feeling, perhaps, that you have made a weak

impression or a blunder of some kind, or a worry about some future date in stress-ful circumstances. You should bear in mind, in dream interpretation, that through the magnifying lens of a developing relationship small-scale anxieties can assume gigantic proportions. For example, if you are renting a car for a day, there is much that can go wrong; but if you plan to use the car on a date, the possibilities for mishap are much more likely to loom large in your mind.

The only way to know whether anxious dreams are reflecting fundamental relationship issues or trivial insecurities is to subject them to close analysis in a spirit of self-inquiry. Deep down in your unconscious you will have recog-nized the potential stumbling blocks in this new adventure, so use the symbols and events of your dreams to prompt searching questions about the kind of future this relationship might hold for you.

In the early days of a relationship it can be difficult to express how we feel. We may try to show our partner how much we care through our actions, but we often hold back from a declaration of love. This is partly because we do not want to frighten our partner away, and partly because we may not entirely trust in the permanence of our feelings. By telling our partner our dreams we can convey our emotions by indirect means — just as dreams themselves do. Think of a dream revelation as being rather like a gift of flowers — unique, beautiful, personal, delicate, and all the more precious for its fleeting evanescence.

The beauty of dream imagery is that its eloquence is virtually infinite. There are only so many ways to express passion or tenderness in words without re-sorting to poetic language which might begin to sound artificial — even if we do not lapse into downright cliché. By sharing dreams, we make up for the poverty of verbal communication, and retain the subtle nuances of meaning that words tend to falsify. In our dream life we are all creative artists, and we can offer our unique works of art as both tokens and expressions of our most pro-found feelings for each other. We may even come to believe that we know each other better, and have become closer, as a result of our dream talk than through our waking conversations.

Describing your dreams to your partner is also a way to prepare the ground for your first physical encounter — a very important step in any relationship. It encourages an ambience of intimacy, which can soften the impact of sexual embrace, placing the physical encounter in the atmosphere of a quieter, more contemplative kind of sharing. If the relationship is destined to flourish, the dreams you have immediately after the first romantic encounter are likely to continue the euphoric excitement of sensuality.

EXERCISE 5

The Treasure of the Self

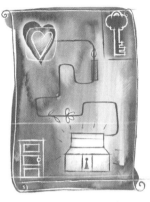

In the early days of a relationship many of us tend to be afflicted with attacks of self-doubt. If the developing bond starts to falter, we all too readily blame ourselves for some error that we think we might have committed. The following exercise is designed to maintain our self-esteem in order to keep the relationship truly on its course.

1. Before you drift off to sleep, imagine a jewel casket. It is in your keeping, but it belongs to your partner, who is the greatest admirer of the treasures it contains. Without ever saying so, they value these treasures more than anything else, and could not bear to part with them under any circumstances.

2. Visualize each treasure in turn: a pearl, a ruby, a gold coin, and a ring. Identify each with the following qualities in yourself: the pearl is the trouble you take to serve your partner (pearl divers put themselves in great danger as they comb the seabed for their booty).

The ruby, an image of full-blooded passion, reflects the depth of your feelings. The gold coin represents a willingness to share what you have – whether material or non-material wealth. And the ring symbolizes your commitment to the relationship.

3. This visualization will unconsciously strengthen your self-esteem and the belief that you have a great deal to offer. In sleep, this sense of self-worth will pass into the unconcious, and may surface in positive dreams, ultimately filling your waking self with new-found strength and confidence.

Erotic Dreams

Sexuality overflows in dreams. Recent surveys estimate that nearly three-quarters of us have had an erotic dream at least once, and many people have them regularly. They are universal, occurring in all cultures, in both genders, and throughout our lifespan. Why then does sex feature so prominently in our dreams? The explanation is that the *libido*, the Freudian term that we use to describe our sex drive, encompasses so much more than purely carnal desire. The libido represents energy, vitality, and spirit; it is the power that drives many of our instincts, including sex and survival. Obviously, energies of such monumental consequence are bound to be vividly and prolifically represented in dreams.

Erotic dreams are the most misunderstood of all, partly because they are so highly charged, and partly because we tend to take them literally — strange images that we would dismiss as unexceptional in any other dream can feel threatening in a sexual context. For example, we might dream of making love to our best friend's partner and, understandably, this might make us feel guilty. In the morning we might feel almost as bad as we would if we had truly committed this act of betrayal. However, sexual imagery, just like any other type, is often symbolic, and dreaming of sex outside a relationship should not be taken to mean that we want to have an affair.

While erotic dreams have many possible explanations, they need never be a source of guilt, embarrassment, or fear. Rather, they afford a healthy way of releasing sexual energy, providing a safe outlet when this energy is not being adequately expressed elsewhere.

Freudian Symbols

When exactly is a dream considered sexual? According to Sigmund Freud (1856–1939), a dream need not contain any obvious sexual activity, or even nudity, to be considered erotic. In fact, dreams whose imagery is overtly sexual are far less common than those in which this content has been disguised. For example, the Freudian dream interpretation of apples or peaches would be that they represent breasts, while the act of climbing a ladder would suggest sexual intercourse, and an airplane would be a reference to male genitalia.

Although Freud had his critics and later psychoanalysts disagreed with his theories, the issue remains controversial. However, we remain deeply indebted to Freud for all his work on dreaming, and the insights into the unconscious mind that his findings provide. Freud remains a powerful influence in psychology today.

Sex dreams are often a barometer of the quality of a relationship at any given time. For example, when we feel that we are not receiving enough emotional nourishment, our sexual dreams may conspicuously lack warmth or affection: we may go through the motions of making love, but feel nothing. But if it is our sexual, rather than emotional, needs that are not being met, we may experience intensely erotic dreams with vivid sensations and overtly arousing images, including ones that would normally leave us unmoved. Similarly, our dreams may become especially erotic when we are struggling to find a sensitive way to ask our partner to try something new in bed.

Quite often, though, sexual dreams are simply to be enjoyed. Any arousing stimuli to which we are exposed during the day may initiate sexual dreams, which can be adventurous and stirring experiences to augment an already satisfying sex life. In telling your partner about your erotic dreams, you may find that you are unwittingly creating just the right conditions for passion, especially if the setting is romantic. Sharing dreams in this way aids the process of getting to know each other in the early stages of a physical relationship — it can be just as enjoyable and relaxing after sex as it is exciting before. But remember that you need to examine erotic dreams in the context of your relationship in order to ascertain whether to enjoy them at face value, or to look for a deeper symbolic meaning.

One of the most enjoyable ways to enhance your sex life is to use erotic dreams as an agenda for the enactment of deeply cherished fantasies. This works best if you agree on the groundrules beforehand. By deciding together that you will share all your erotic dreams shortly after you have experienced them, and then take a vote together on which ones to act out, you remove the burden of individual responsibility. The theory is that, this way, it will be easier for you to dodge the inhibition or embarrassment that normally prevents you from saying what you really want. Lovers have been known to cheat by pretending to have had a particular erotic dream in the hope that their partner will act it out — although dishonesty is not to be encouraged, this is only harmless fun.

When you use dreams in this way as fantasy enactment cues, anything is permissible so long as it is consensual. If you or your partner begins to feel uncomfortable, just call a halt to the proceedings and forget the episode ever happened. Another basic rule is that neither party should ever be blamed for strange or outlandish proposals. However, avoid at all costs games of violence that involve actual hurt and pain — they can only lead to heartbreak in the end.

EXERCISE 6

The Dream Pillow Book

A novel way to add sparkle to your sex life is to share erotic dreams with your partner by recording them in a Dream Pillow Book — a type of bedroom journal once used by Japanese courtesans, among others. You may find that this exercise unleashes a creative burst of uninhibited fantasies unlike anything you would normally experience in waking reality.

I. Begin by inventing an erotic story, perhaps using part of a recent sexual dream as a starting point, and record the story in a special bedtime dream book. Choose whatever setting, images, characters, and storyline you like — anything you imagine might appeal to your partner. Sprinkle your story generously with descriptions of what you see, hear, feel, smell, and taste, in as much detail as possible.

2. Give the book to your partner, perhaps by leaving it on their pillow — the idea is that they read your story before falling asleep. The goal, of course, is to prompt an erotic dream, but if they find themselves becoming aroused while reading, so much the better!

3. Next day, your partner uses whatever fragments of their sexual dreams they can recall to write the next installment of your ongoing erotic saga. Expect the unexpected — their dream consciousness will probably add its own titillating twist to the tale.

4. Pass the Dream Pillow Book back and forth, between you, day by day, for as long as you wish. Each new account that you add will build on the excitement of the one before.

Perennial Love

Binding love is that special state of a mature relationship when stability, familiarity, and fulfillment have taken deep root. Key ingredients are intimacy, passion, and commitment. Intimacy can be defined as emotional bonding; passion is the satisfaction of the physical, with elements also of nurturing and self-assertion; and commitment is a conscious decision of attachment — the bond that keeps a relationship together during hard times. Together, these three components complete a triangle that links two people in a lasting and fulfilling union.

An apparently stable relationship can drift imperceptibly into a bundle of niggling discontents — you can wake up to unhappiness one morning without knowing how you arrived there. A healthy relationship, on the other hand, tackles key issues in good time to prevent them from turning the atmosphere of the relationship sour, while at the same time accepting that some differences of opinion or temperament must simply be accepted and respected.

Dreams can help you to monitor your relationship regularly to ensure that any difficulties are recognized and brought out into the open. All three sides of the intimacy/passion/commitment triangle are fit subjects for such inspection. You might decide to do dreamwork on each of these in turn at specific intervals — one per month, say, so that each dimension receives a quarterly review in which you look back over that quarter's dreams. Or you might prefer to round up all three dimensions in one big session, which might be monthly or quarterly (with corresponding qualifying periods for the

EXERCISE 7

Tending the Garden

Love is like a plant. You cannot merely accept it and stow it away in a closet, or just leave it to fend for itself. If you want your plant to flourish, you have to give it some attention. Use the following pre-sleep visualization to keep your relationship garden alive in your imagination, and in your dreams.

I. As you fall asleep, visualize your relationship as a beautiful garden. Recall how this garden cast a spell on you, and how you first tilled its soil and planted the seeds of love.

2. Picture yourself in your garden, which is divided into three areas: intimacy, passion, and commitment. Admire the features in each: intimacy has exquisite tiny flowers; passion has big, bright blooms; commitment has practical plants such as herbs. Recall how you weeded out problems, and how you watered your relationship garden with faith, as well as love and support.

3. Now do your tour again, closely inspecting what is growing. Are all the plants and flowers healthy and strong? Have any weeds started to grow? If so, identify their character and imagine uprooting them.

4. Before you sleep, imagine yourself rising into the air and looking down on the garden. Meditate on the pattern it makes. If you dream that night of growth, nature, landscape, nurturing, water, paths, trees, or flowers (all symbols to which the dreaming mind commonly resorts), try to interpret this in the light of your relationship garden.

dreams you choose to examine). Of course, it is not necessary to be so systematic if you prefer not to be committed to a fixed curriculum: you could instead respond to mood or inclination. Be sure at each session to check the emotional temperature of your dreams as well as the symbolism. Look out in particular for fractures, rifts, or tensions in your dream narratives – but be alert also to positive symbols, which can be useful in providing mutual reassurance. A dream diary is a vital tool in such a relationship maintenance program. A couple who have been together for years may feel that each knows all there is to know about the other. Dream dialogues (see pp.76–9) provide a salutary corrective to this unnecessarily gloomy view of relationships: there will always be both dreams and interpretations that catch you unawares, because the unconscious, like the universe, is of infinite extent. This in turn means that your relationship is inexhaustible in its possibilities.

In a mature relationship there will inevitably come a time when one partner needs to give the other focused support – perhaps in response to serious illness, the death of a family member or close friend, or a crisis at work. Dreamwork can be especially helpful in such circumstances. Bear in mind that illness can generate its own disturbing dream images, and the best way to deal with these is often to counter them with more soothing influences – tell your partner about any dreams of growth or renewal you have had. Much the same can be said for bereavement. When someone close to your partner dies, or any external crisis strikes, suspend the dreamwork that you are conducting on concerns within the relationship, to

Remembering Special Occasions

It is something of a cliché that husbands forget anniversaries and their wives' birthdays, but slips of memory can affect us all. Using dream remembrance cues can help bring those vital dates to mind.

One of the best ways to use dreams to remind us of special occasions is to select a symbol and associate it with an important date. For example, you could visualize your partner as a giant balloon with the date inscribed across its side, or as a racehorse with the number corresponding to the birthday or anniversary displayed on its saddle. The more imaginative the image, the more memorable it will be.

Well in advance of the target date, you need to focus on the image every night, before going to sleep. Try to keep this up regularly, and after a while you should notice the symbol you selected to remind you of your special date occuring in your dreams.

concentrate instead on stimulating dreams of strength and healing to help your partner through this difficult time.

Dream diaries, over the course of a long-term relationship, become a unique record of the ups and downs of a partnership — imagine the excitement of discovering a dream log that your parents maintained throughout their marriage. Use your archives regularly to trace continuities of theme and symbol that have threaded through your dreams over the years. As you age together, your dream selves may retain their youthful vigor and enthusiasm, but equally they will grow in the richness of accumulated experiences, and your diaries will confirm that dream symbolism becomes more revealing and complex as time goes by.

Conquering Jealousy

Once perceived as a dark aspect of love, jealousy is regarded nowadays as a primitive and sometimes destructive emotion. Many of us are reluctant to admit to being jealous, but it is actually a commonly experienced feeling, in both waking reality and dreams. It usually stems from a fear of loss. Our instinctive reaction to fear is to fight (or flee), so it is understandable that intense jealousy can cause us to lash out, physically or verbally, especially if we think that our relationship is under threat.

Jealousy is an emotion particularly suited to expression in the language of dreams — it has a primeval quality that is thoroughly in tune with the unconscious. It often appears undisguised in dreams, especially if we are possessive by nature or insecure in our relationship. The strength of feeling comes in part from the sense of usurpation: another is in our place, and we feel that our self-worth — even perhaps our identity — is seriously threatened. Also, we hate not to know, because that forces us to imagine, and our imaginings usually encompass the worst possible scenario. The urge to know comes partly because we long, self-destructively, to know the worst and partly because we want to be proven wrong. So jealousy is both complex and contradictory, which is why it eats away so effectively at the foundations of our relationship and destroys our peace of mind.

People who are jealous by temperament tend to exaggerate the other's offense — often it is all in their minds, stemming from a deep-rooted insecurity. Even when there has actually been some unfaithfulness, we have to work through and

Waving the Past Goodbye

Unfaithfulness is one of the most devas-  it clear that neither of you has anything
tating things that can happen in a re- to hide. If the "intruder" appears in a
lationship. If it is accepted as just an dream, the innocent one should not be
aberration (for example, a brief affair or too alarmed or despondent — it is natur-
a temporary attraction), and the wronged al that someone who has created such
party is forgiving, dreams can be helpful in the process a disturbance in the relationship should manifest
of healing. themselves in dream life, even though this person no

The key to reviving the relationship is to rebuild the longer plays a part as flesh and blood. In time, if all
trust that has been compromised between you. Telling is well within the reconciled relationship, the ghost will
each other your dreams on a regular basis can make begin to fade.

beyond our jealousy — difficult as this will be — before we can deal with the situation
in a way that brings about the best outcome.

One way to enlist the help of dreams is the technique of substitution. Let us
say that we have dreamed of our partner walking arm in arm with our rival (imaginary or otherwise) along a seafront, and that intense feelings of hurt are stirred by
the scenario. The following night, before going to sleep, we might consciously
imagine ourselves substituted for the rival; we visualize the weight of our partner's
arm resting cosily against ours, and the tang of the sea breeze. In other words, we
are using our conscious mind to affirm our sense of what is right, just as our unconscious, in the previous night's dream, affirmed the opposite. Such affirmations
can help to rid our dreams of their jealousy.

Conflict and Confusion

Even in the most solid relationship, conflicts and confusions are bound to arise from time to time. They are an inevitable byproduct of the chemistry between two human beings with distinct personalities, separate histories, and conflicting needs, as well as different attitudes and opinions. With so many diverse factors to balance, is it any wonder that clashes occur? All couples in strong relationships fight, but they also know *how* to fight and to fight healthily.

Tensions that occur within a relationship often build up insidiously. They are usually sparked by a small incident or disagreement, but if left unresolved hurt feelings can swell and gnaw away at the very fabric of intimacy. Clashes can also be exacerbated by outside pressures. For example, parents who disapprove of their offspring's choice of partner can put untold strain on the relationship by creating a conflict of loyalties. This is where confusion rears its head: pulled in opposite directions, our mind starts to experience patterns of interference that blur its usual clarity — like radio waves jammed by a foreign transmitter.

All relationships experience periods of distance and doubt as well as closeness and contentment. Conflict is seldom terminal, and two or three conversations are usually enough to restore normality. Of course, some conflicts go deeper and can threaten long-term disruption to mutual harmony. Both trivial and severe forms of conflict are susceptible to constructive dreamwork.

At an unconscious level, dreams may offer automatic help in providing an outlet for excess anger or frustration, although the precise workings of this compensation process are little understood.

68

EXERCISE 8

The Oracle of Touch

Relationship problems often respond to a special dream incubation or prompting technique known as kinesthetic dreaming. *This method can be used to address specific challenges such as taking steps toward a compromise on a divisive issue. Although your partner is required in the exercise, they need not be aware of the planned incubation.*

1. Decide what exactly you wish to achieve through your incubation. For example, formulate and focus on a specific question or request to help you find a resolution to a particular conflict with your partner. Do not make the question or request too complicated.

2. As you relax together at bedtime, offer to give your partner a massage to help them sleep. Caress and rub them gently, and as you do so, silently "talk" to each part of their body, asking the question or making the request that you devised earlier. Feel your partner's skin beneath your fingers and fix a memory of the sensation in your mind.

3. Now thank each part of your partner's body for what it means to you – their hands for a caring touch, their back for strength, their arms for holding you, and so on.

4. When you have finished the massage, allow yourself to drift off to sleep holding in your mind the memory of your touch on your partner's skin.

5. Search your dreams for guidance – they may suggest why the problem has arisen or help you to see your partner's viewpoint, and so give you insight into how best to reconcile your differences.

You could try to aid the unconscious in its corrective activities by prompting dreams of release and letting the psychological discharge operate while you sleep. For example, before going to bed at night meditate on crashing waves, a bursting dam, or a geyser sending its waters sky-high. The hope is that such imagery will generate "cathartic" dreams that will restore balance to your feelings, purging them of aggressions that have accumulated from the past, and that are perhaps not relevant to the current situation.

Where the waking mind fails to make headway on the question of how to resolve conflict or confusion, dreams can help by providing a fresh set of images and events by which we can take our bearings. Work through these dreams either alone or with your partner, and, with the help of these signposts, try to establish some constructive ways to move forward out of the storm.

When conflicts generate negative emotions, the worst thing we can do is brood over them in solitude. Scan your dreams for clues about how to respond in a more active way. If your dreams seem to offer only negative answers, there are various approaches you can try. One is to establish in your mind, or on paper, a scenario that is exactly the opposite of the one in your dream, and use this as a focus for meditation – especially just prior to sleep. Another is to interpret the dream's negativity as a warning from your unconscious about the dangerous tendencies you are showing – a billboard poster showing how things might be unless you take change into your own hands. There are also many ways in which you might be able to achieve a breakthrough by mutual dreamwork.

Some conflicts and confusions upset us more deeply than we recognize in our conscious minds. If such problems erupt into a dream in a flood of disturbing

Picking up the Pieces

After a quarrel, even one that is resolved in a satisfactory fashion for both parties, there will usually be an atmosphere of unease or awkwardness that takes a little while to go away — depending on your temperaments and how you spend your time together.

Your dreams for the next night or so may not "understand" that the conflict has been healed: in other words, they may be slightly out of date. This often happens when the dispute has centered around some fundamental issue or difference of opinion. Always feel that you are free to ignore your dreams if you think there is a chance that they may not yet have caught up with waking events. Bear this possibility in mind while scanning your dreams carefully for positive confimation that your reconciliation is whole-hearted and that no trace of resentment lingers.

images, it is usually constructive to tell your partner about the dream soon afterward. Explain that it has shown how you have been disguising the true extent of your unhappiness even from yourself. By following this method, you can use the dream as a direct introduction to a subject of conversation that would otherwise be hard to broach.

You may find that you do not even have to comment on your disturbing dream to your partner because they immediately understand its emotional truth, and may even have similar dreams of their own to report to you in turn. When this happens, you have won half the battle — once the problems have been isolated and agreed, resolving them is really just a matter of deciding what course of action to take by working through them in constructive and sympathetic conversations.

Swansong

Few experiences are as emotionally taxing, if not outright traumatic, as the ending of a relationship. Even when it is our own decision to call things to a halt, the situation is nearly always fraught with pain; and often this is mixed with conflict and bitterness.

At times of parting, dreams can bolster our strength and renew our hopes for the future. If the relationship was truly flawed, you might even find that your dreams seem to rejoice in the prospect of a rescued future. Images of liberation, open spaces, exhilarating physical exercise, or magical transformations, can all be taken as signs that you or your partner have taken the right step. If no such images appear, one approach would be to attempt to conjure them into your dreams by affirmations prior to sleep. Using this method you can stimulate revitalizing dreams of perseverance, emotional stability, and empowerment. Affirmations can work well in triads — for example, you might say softly to your-

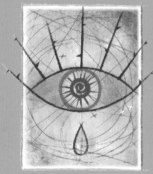

self before drifting off to sleep: "I seek the wisdom to recognize my path; I seek the courage to follow my path; I seek the strength to persevere on my path." The same affirmations would be appropriate at various stages in the parting process: you could use them before making the final break, or to see you through a series of painful discussions, as well as when trying hard not to contact your ex-partner.

The Miraculous Leap of Faith

Letting go of a relationship often requires a leap of faith, especially when we know we must walk away but find it hard to summon up the courage to do so. This is especially true if the relationship has been longlasting: no matter how unsatisfying we find the situation, the prospect of a protracted parting, with all the bafflement and recriminations it might bring, acts as a strong deterrent. In order to come through the ordeal, we must believe that what lies ahead on our path will be worth all the pain endured to get there. Dreams can offer reassurance at such times, particularly if we consciously prompt them by using affirmations.

One dreamer, who had resigned herself to never loving again in the aftermath of a divorce that had battered her self-esteem, incubated a miracle dream to re-establish her faith in love. First, she repeated to herself the simple affirmation, "I can walk on clouds," which made her feel alive and invigorated. That night she dreamed that she stood gripping the head of a lion gargoyle at the top of Nôtre Dame Cathedral in Paris. She stared out over the city and then closed her eyes, held her breath, and slowly stepped out into midair. She was not at all surprised when she did not fall. She remained suspended in the air for a moment as she contentedly watched the city bustling below, before gently floating to the ground. This amazing dream feat restored her hope in the future.

To incubate your own miracle dream before you fall asleep, imagine that you are performing an impossible feat with incredible ease – perhaps walking on water, or dousing a forest fire just by looking at the flames, or riding an untamable wild horse. If this fails the first time, do not be discouraged or take it as a negative sign – just keep trying and you may soon succeed in working your own dream miracle.

Working Together

*D*reams provide a unique opportunity to work with your partner to help your relationship grow, and to heal it when it becomes sick. The inherent candor and wisdom of dreams teach us to understand and define our own needs and aspirations better, as well as gain a deeper appreciation of those of our lover.

In this chapter we will explore how sharing our dreams with our partner can open a mutually reinforcing dialogue through role play, storytelling, and co-dreaming. We will examine how the intrinsic ambiguity of dreams can give us unexpected insights into each other, as well as teaching us to how to work together to break down barriers (emotional, psychological, and/or physical), release resentment, inspire hope, and arouse desire. There are several exercises that you can undertake with your partner, ranging from the purely playful to the more psychologically challenging, but they are all designed to build on the existing strengths of our relationships and iron out the inevitable weaknesses.

Dream Dialogues

A dream recalled in waking life is like a stranger in a strange land. It needs help to make its way into the full light of consciousness without being misunderstood. By working alone on your dreams, using their mood and their symbolism as touchstones to assess your emotional life, you will be able to illuminate and enrich many aspects of your most cherished relationship. However, imagine how much more progress you could make if you involved your partner (or a friend) as a co-worker. As with two alchemists in a laboratory together, your chances of stumbling across the secret of transforming base metal into gold will be dramatically increased by mutual assistance.

It makes sense to develop dream dialogue techniques in stages, from the simplest toward the more sophisticated. First, accustom yourselves to just talking through your dreams, and trying to establish some possible meanings. In doing this, even if you find yourselves unable to make much progress with interpretation, you will acclimatize to the basic language of self-analysis, and grow used to talking about your emotions, gradually ridding yourself of any inhibitions. Work on key symbols with the dream oracle in this book to explore possible meanings together (see pp.136–9). After a few weeks or so of regular work you can expect to feel that you are making some headway, at least in your ability to communicate, as you try to make sense of the mysteries of dreaming.

Later you might go on to try a question-and-answer approach rather than an unstructured dialogue. As the listener, ask about the moods and

EXERCISE 9

Sharing a Dream Journal

A shared dream journal is an effective way to keep a dialogue going between two dreamers. You could simply add to it whenever the occasion arises, or you could write up your entries during dream dialogues together. The same approach could be followed by two friends, or even by a whole family.

1. Use one journal between both partners. This book is owned equally by both of you, so it cannot contain individual secrets.

2. For clarity, begin all new entries on a fresh page, putting the date and dreamer's name at the top (or you could each use a different-colored ink).

3. Write a synopsis of your dream, trying not to be overly wordy. Remember that the most important messages from a dream are contained in its emotions and symbolism, so make sure that you cover these aspects particularly thoroughly.

4. You might choose to work on the interpretation together, writing down key words at the end of your entry. Or you could run two parallel interpretation columns down the page – allowing each of you to work alone on your own interpretations without being influenced by the other (especially if you mask off any comments your partner has already made).

5. Read and discuss the dream journal regularly, and before sleep meditate on the symbols recorded there. You might find that they stimulate further dreams incorporating the same raw material.

feelings that dream events invoked in the dreamer — either at the time or now, in recollection. Ask about the details — what color was such and such a feature, how precisely did such and such a character register their emotion? Ask also about how the dream felt from the point of view of apparently significant inanimate objects in the dream — how would the trees have felt as the wind was rustling through them, and so on. This is, in some ways, a form of role play (see p.94), with a dreamer and an interrogator. The playacting element helps to liberate the imagination and also makes the exercise more fun to do.

In dream dialogues it is important to delve into the emotional overtones of any symbols you identify together. Try to go beyond merely neutral descriptions of a scene or narrative. For example, if your partner begins by recalling them-selves zipping through the air astride a cartoon missile that was about to explode, be sure to ask how this made them feel. They might reply that it was exhilarating, like flying at the speed of light — they had never felt more alive. At this point you might each free-associate around the symbol, making two separate sets of notes, which you can then compare. This might yield something like the following: "missile" leads to rocket, launch, fast, unstoppable; "explosion" to dynamite, fire, burning, danger, harm; "speed of light" to stars, spaceship, flying, fun. Any of these terms could then be fruitfully explored in a discussion about your relationship. In particular, explore the ambiguities and paradoxes that surround most symbols: dynamite, for example, is destructive but the word is also used colloquially as a term of approbation. All relationships are riddled with ambiguity and paradox, and these qualities will often be directly mirrored in your dream symbols.

EXERCISE 10

A Communion of Symbols

This exercise shows how the symbols of one person's dreams can inspire and clarify the symbols of the other's — a process called symbiotic symbolism. *Jungian theory offers two possible explanations of this technique: one dream is incubating the next, by association; or there is unconscious communication between the dreamers through the symbols of the collective unconscious — the universal imagery that is encoded in all our brains.*

1. Partner A describes, in the morning, the dream they have had during the night, paying particular attention to any symbols that appeared — images loaded with special meaning or those that provoke the strongest emotions. These might be images of nature, or methods of transport, or even everyday objects — the possibilities are endless — but usually the symbols will be familiar and easily recognizable.

2. Both partners talk through the symbols, and free-associate around them. For example, a dream featuring sunflowers might spark off associations with Van Gogh (who often painted them), which might in turn suggest an art gallery. Finally, the couple return to the original dream symbol that has proven most fruitful in its associations, and both meditate on this symbol before sleeping.

3. The next day it is Partner B's turn to recount their dream and follow steps 1 and 2. If both partners have dreams on a particular night, the two dreams are looked at in turn, and the two most prominent symbols — one from each dream — are made the object of pre-sleep meditation.

Talking and Listening

Listening, understanding, and self-expression form the bedrock of any relationship. We take these skills for granted because we use them in conversation every day — through words and observations. It is almost impossible not to communicate with others, but to do so effectively — without hasty judgment or prejudice — is significantly more complex than it may at first appear.

How often have you attributed a belief, mood, or thought to a lover based solely on a snippet of their body language? Or to a friend from their facial expression? The trouble with non-verbal communication, and the assumptions we make from it, is that by the law of probability we are sometimes bound to jump to the wrong conclusions, and in so doing, respond by saying or doing the wrong thing, or by feeling an inappropriate emotion.

How can our dreams help? For a start, when we enter into a dream dialogue with another person, we create a slightly detached platform from which to improve our abilities to listen and understand (by being detached we are less likely to be drawn into an emotive, and unconstructive, discussion). An incisive analysis of the meanings of another person's dream requires concentration, understanding, and articulation. And these are the same skills that we need in everyday life to ensure that we are communicating effectively with the people closest to us.

In addition, when there is a communication breakdown in our waking lives, our dreams often present the first warning signs — if we are able to see the problem coming, it is easier to keep daily life in perspective. When our nighttime visions

EXERCISE 11

The Tapestry of Meaning

*An illuminating dialogue may take the form of a **dream dialectic** — an interpretation by one is supplemented by an insight from the other to build up a composite picture, to which the first partner reacts, and so on. As listener, prevent personal associations from influencing you, and try to visualize aspects of the dream that the other person describes.*

I. As the dreamer describes the dream, make believe that you are listening to a poetic monologue on the radio, as if the images are being spun out of an imagination unknown to you. (It may help if you sit back to back for this.)

2. While listening, your aim is to absorb all the details and nuances of your partner's dream experience. During pauses ask open questions ("How did you feel …?" not "Did you feel scared?"; or "Who might the stranger have been?" not "Was it your boss?"). Try not to ask questions, or prompt answers, about possible meanings.

3. Once you have gleaned all the information you can from the dreamer, consider possible interpretations and tell the dreamer why you came to these conclusions. The dreamer should listen without interrupting you, and should save questions for your natural pauses. When you have finished, it is the dreamer's turn to interpret the dream, drawing upon your findings as well as their own.

4. Keep listening and relating in this way, until, between you, you have built up a composite analysis of the dream's meaning, on which you both agree.

are riddled with symbols of collapse or destruction, such as bombs and other explosive devices, we can take it as a warning that somewhere in our lives our communication skills are not functioning as they should. Sometimes the symbols are a little more subtle. For example, if you dream of being under-water, bear in mind that this is an environment in which communication is difficult; and if you dream of being an astronaut, the key to the symbolism may be the helmet, which hinders speech, rather than more obvious interpret-ations such as the exhilarating sense of weightlessness or the liberating feeling of transcending boundaries.

Virtually any form of mutual dreamwork is going to help communication between you and your partner. However, there are certain basic principles con-cerned with talking and listening effectively that both of you should master.

A common mistake when relating a dream is to convey just the highlights, which once they have been described aloud tend to be all that you subsequently remember. This is rather similar to the phenomenon whereby it is the photo-graphs of our childhood we remember, rather than the actual events: in other words, what is fixed in the process of recording tends to overshadow or even obliterate what is left out. In telling a dream for the first time, therefore, we should be sure that we proceed slowly and reflectively, trying hard not to omit anything. To do this it is helpful to be in a setting that is comfortable and in no way distracting. You might play gentle music quietly in the background, but try to avoid any sounds that might make it harder to concentrate on your dream. Avoid the temptation to organize your dream, to fill in gaps with invented bridge passages, or to overdramatize. Remember that your aim is not to entertain or amaze your partner, but to bring about closer understanding.

Trying all the Angles

After talking about a dream, try to explore its associations from as many viewpoints as possible. By way of an example, if gold coins appear in your dream there are various possible levels on which you can describe them, as itemized below. As a listener, be alert to these possibilities and save up your comments and questions. Make sure that no stone is left unturned.

Literal

Gold coins are obvious indications of wealth, spending power, or finances. When describing a dream, make it clear whether you perceived the gold coins purely as money, or as a means to an end. When listening, ask a question such as, "How might you spend them?"

Symbolic

The coins may represent a less tangible value. Perhaps they are the object of some kind of quest – perhaps even for happiness in your relationship, or, in some circumstances, for independence. When describing the dream, make it clear whether the coins excited any feelings of yearning or unsatisfied potential. When listening, remember to ask questions about what feelings the coins evoked in the dreamer.

Associative

Always bear in mind the physical characteristics of the elements that appear in a dream. Gold coins are round and yellow, and hence like the sun. Perhaps they symbolize a more natural, carefree way of life? Or perhaps you associate the coins with a particular place or event? If, as a dreamer, any similes occur to you in your dream narrative, be sure to take note of them – they may be important. When listening, always ask questions about resemblances, such as, "What other things did the coins remind you of?"

Weaving Stories

One of the most fascinating and cutting-edge methods of interpretive dreamwork involves transforming dream stories into waking narratives. This is a powerful form of dream role play that allows you and your partner to explore the middle ground between the conscious and unconscious, to bring to the surface unconscious fears or other difficulties in order to face up to them, or to rewrite troublesome dreams. Developing dream stories helps you build up self-esteem, and encourages intimacy with your partner, bringing cohesion to the relationship. Using this method, you can work together with your partner to isolate your emotional and behavioral weak spots and shore them up in ways that side-step defensive psychological barriers.

The simplest application of this form of role play is dream extension, where a dream scenario is acted out, in the form of a dialogue, beyond its conclusion, or that conclusion is modified. Let us consider an example. Brian dreamed that he was chasing a monster which was ready to attack his partner, Kim. He heard her screaming for his help and he tried to reach her, but as he approached, he was paralyzed and could not move even the smallest muscle. Suddenly the screaming stopped, and there was silence. There was no trace of either Kim or the monster. He felt terrible, helpless, and guilty — a complete failure. Then he woke up.

In the extension exercise, Brian and Kim both assume their dream roles but improvise an alternative ending. The two partners take it in turn to describe events. Brian keeps chasing the monster,

Mutual Daydreaming

Nearly everyone has daydreams, whether at home, at work, or in the classroom — any time or anywhere. These waking fantasies span the entire range of human experience, from work tasks and home activities to adventurous escapes and erotic encounters.

Daydreams fall within a state of awareness that psychologists call a *differentiated waking state*, which is somewhere between active consciousness and sleep. Most of us have also experienced the intensely colorful images and exaggerated sense of reality of daydreams which occur as we drift out of sleep — known as *hypnopompic hallucinations*. But their most interesting feature is that, unlike nighttime dreams, they are under the control of our will. They can be used as a mutual exercise whereby two partners, perhaps lying in bed together, contribute equally to the daydream and use it to explore themes that are of shared concern.

The kernel of the fantasy may come from either of you, but the unfolding process is mutual and spontaneous. Each partner contributes to the free-flow to create a winding progression of images, twisting and turning in unpredictable ways, governed by the unconscious mind. As the daydream evolves, you both project unconscious material into the fantasy, to reveal feelings and attitudes that may be hidden from conscious awareness.

We can also manipulate a daydream through a process analogous to dream incubation, to progress a relationship. For example, if, in your fantasy, you come to a halt in a difficult scene or you feel defenseless or vulnerable, take control of the daydream and deliberately develop the characters or plot in such a way as to bring about a more positive outcome.

Afterward, talk with your partner in a more conscious way about the story that developed — as if it were a true dream. You might wish to return to some of the themes or images later in the day (over a candlelit dinner, perhaps) or keep a mutual diary (see p.77).

but when he feels the paralysis is about to set in, he screams at the horrible creature with all his might. This causes Kim to stop yelling as she is taken by surprise
and temporarily distracted — for a moment she thinks about Brian and not the
monster. Brian continues to scream until the monster turns to face him instead
of his partner. He finds a flashlight in his coat pocket and shines the beam right
in the monster's face. Kim asks him what the monster looks like and Brian
remarks that it has her father's eyes. The dream monster then cowers, leaving
them both alone. Kim can now declare that she feels safe, and they hug each other.
Acting this dream scenario was empowering for them both, as it liberated them
from the specter of Kim's father, who had never approved of their marriage.

Role play like Brian and Kim's can be an effective tool to tame nightmares —
frightening dreams that have no resolution because the dreamer wakes up in
terror. If you experience a nightmare, try acting it out with your partner, but
when the dream ends, keep going and improvise until you reach a conclu-

sion. If it ends in fear, as is almost always the case, face up to this
fear, do not cower from it. Perhaps fish out a flashlight as Brian
did, recognizing that terror thrives in the dark and that shedding
light exposes, weakens, and ultimately destroys the threat.

There are countless variations of role-play technique, based on developing a
story from the dream's subtext. For example, partners can shift roles in a dream,
each re-enacting it from the other's perspective — an exercise that offers an
insight into what your partner is feeling. Alternatively, you might take on the role
of a non-human element, and then retell the dream from its perspective. The
improvisations gain a momentum of their own — sometimes surprising, sometimes unsettling, but always revealing new aspects of your relationship.

The Director's Cut

Most people would relish the chance to direct their own movie, and through the technique of dream scriptwork, you can. This playful yet searching and insightful way to act out a fantasy allows you to set the scene, steam up the plot, inspire exciting characters, and write your own ending, using your imagination to deepen the connection with your lover.

1. Choose a dream that seems rich in action or imagery — there need be no obvious connection with your relationship.

2. Next, act out several versions of the dream using "what if?" scenarios. What if the angel flying over your house landed in your backyard? What if you hitched a ride on the angel's back? How would even a minor change affect the story?

3. After running through the whole story once, imagine that you are co-directors of the movie, trying to put on the best possible version — the "director's cut." Choose the most insightful scenarios — the ones that strike you intuitively as "true."

4. Run through the action with dialogue. Each of you should direct the other to get the best performance — making suggestions for changes to make the drama more effective.

5. After creating the final version for your relationship studio, enact the role of co-teachers in a movie masterclass and plan how you would explain the psychological meanings of the movie to film students.

Shared Dreaming

Dreams are egocentric, prodigiously selfish, and fiercely protective of our individual needs and desires. Yet in any meaningful relationship, one person's feelings, anxieties, hopes, and concerns will significantly overlap with the other's — like two perspectives on the same object, distinct but recognizably alike.

We are sometimes tempted to think that some couples inhabit not two minds but one. They seem to echo each other's thoughts, have the same reactions to new experiences, take pleasure in the same things, and, with other people, talk all the time about "we" — as if they no longer have individual opinions about anything and the pronoun "I" has become obsolete!

Of course, there can be no such thing as a shared mind, only shared thoughts. Nevertheless, it is true that couples are more likely to think like each other than are mere acquaintances or strangers (although similar coincidences of feeling or opinion are often found among friends or work colleagues). This is not only to do with the fact that people who form relationships tend already to be like-minded in some respect and usually have common interests of some sort: it is also a reflection of time spent together in mutual experiences, and of questions that need to be resolved to the satisfaction of each: where shall we live? where shall we go on vacation? which friends shall we visit together? how can we be happy together? how can we adjust to accommodate each other's most cherished wishes?

Given this background of mental affinity, it is interesting to try some dream experiments to see if you can reach together the much-sought goal of shared

dreaming – that is, each party to the relationship enjoying, simultaneously, the same dream, or a dream in the same setting. The ultimate dream-sharing achievement is meeting by pre-arrangement in a dream, at an agreed place. Such a goal is highly elusive, but one reward for trying is the possibility along the way of less extreme forms of dream sharing – for example, perhaps a shared symbol, or two symbols that complement each other.

Let us start with the less ambitious forms of dream affinity and progress up the ladder to the giddy heights of true co-dreaming. First, there is the idea of working together on two dreams, each experienced by one of the partners during the same night. These dreams may be very different indeed, but it is a fascinating and entertaining exercise to try to weave a single story out of the two scenarios. This process will tax your imagination, and lead to some highly incongruous and surreal juxtapositions. Yet because dreams are often incongruous and surreal in any case, there is little danger that the composite dream you create together will not seem realistically dreamlike. Look for continuities of theme and symbolism. However, if you find no such links, perhaps this very difference between the two dreams will be a fruitful subject to explore together. Does it reveal any differences in the ways in which you each approach life? Does it expose any predictable gender differences? Does it suggest divergent perspectives on key issues within your relationship?

It may be possible to give a focus to such dream comparisons by prompting both of you to dream about a particular symbol or setting – perhaps one that has occurred in your dreams before. Meditate together on this symbol before sleep, and in the morning see whether it has surfaced during the night in the dreams of both partners. An exercise like this tends to have a high failure rate, but do not be discouraged from trying. A successful attempt to share a dream symbol can be almost ecstatically rewarding, confirming that you have the ability to reach great heights of empathy together. You might choose a symbol that already has special significance for both of you, or one that is pertinent to certain current issues – for example, a house if you are contemplating living together, or a baby if you are wondering whether to start a family, or even a rainforest if you have strong views about conserving the environment.

Unfortunately, shared dreaming has proven impossible to reproduce under experimental conditions. However, many credible reports have been documented. Anthropologists who study primitive peoples such as the Senoi of Malaysia report that it is not uncommon for entire villages to experience the same dream simultaneously.

Twins in Peril

Some of the most convincing accounts of shared dreams have been experienced by identical twins. Just after Louise and her twin sister Rachel had moved out of the parental home and were living apart for the first time, Louise dreamed that she had shrunk in size and was locked inside a doll's house. As she tried desperately to escape, she heard Rachel scream and saw her run out of the room, chased by a menacing shadow. Louise felt small and totally powerless. That night, Rachel had the same nightmare except that in her dream, she was the one locked inside a doll's house, while Louise was chased by a shadow. The girls concluded that their dreams simply reflected each twin's anxiety about coping alone. Although scientific research suggests that identical twins are able to communicate telepathically, this does not fully explain the remarkable symmetry of the two dreams.

Once you have made headway with some of the less ambitious methods of dream sharing, it is time to try for the ultimate goal of true co-dreaming. If you feel discouraged at any time by a lack of results, bear in mind that it takes only one successful dream rendezvous to make up for months of trying to no avail.

Decide on a meeting-place that has positive associations for you both — or somewhere especially beautiful that you have visited together. Spend time talking about the place and reliving your shared memories. Visualize the chosen location often, capturing its qualities in a spoken description, and look at photographs if you have them. On the night of the dream rendezvous each of you should speak aloud an affirmation that you will meet at this place (be as specific as you can) in sleep. Have faith: nothing undermines success so much as skepticism.

A Bird in the Nest

Case Study

Dreams are often enigmatic in their symbolism, but occasionally they point the way with unexpected clarity. This case study focuses on a couple whose mutual dreamwork blessed them with clear signposts toward parenthood.

Mark and Mary were trying to decide whether or not to have a baby. They vacillated from having an urgent desire for a child to coming down definitely against the idea because they feared their freedom would be lost. For several years they hoped that their dilemma would be resolved but no matter how much they believed that one day a solution would present itself, this did not happen. Their friends suggested that they just go ahead and start a family, advising them that, although many couples go through the same uncertainties, these are soon resolved once a child is conceived. However, Mark and Mary were reluctant to follow such counsel.

Mark and Mary had done some individual dream interpretation in the past but had never attempted any co-operative dreamwork. They began with a series of dream incubations, starting with the simple but crucial question, "Should we have a baby?"

Mary was first to respond to the incubation. Her dream turned out to be surprisingly straightforward — it showed an empty baby-carrier, which prompted feelings of sadness. (This was by no means the first of Mary's "baby" dreams, as the couple called them — she had experienced several during the years in which they had struggled to reach a decision.) She believed that this most recent dream reflected the emptiness she would in the end experience if they decided against having a child.

Using the image of the empty baby-carrier as a stimulus, the following night Mark dreamed that he was running down a narrow, dimly lit street, dodging children who begged him for money as he chased after a missing, and ultimately irretrievable, clock. His dream emotions felt desperately sad. Mark interpreted his dream initially as a warning that he would experience regret over the time that he and Mary had already lost, if they now chose to go ahead and have a child. But after discussing the symbolism together, the couple realized that it could also represent a sorrowful sense that time was running out — the clock was, in part, "biological."

Using Mark's symbols as further prompts, one night Mary dreamed of cuddling and comforting an injured animal that had found its way into a watchmaker's store. Mark's final "baby" dream, using Mary's injured animal as an incubation stimulus, featured a healthy bird chick that sang happily in their house. The couple linked the bird with nesting and nurture. As both their dreams felt happy, Mark and Mary finally made the momentous decision to go ahead and try for their baby.

Dream Role Play

Dream role play is a method of acting out a dream when you are awake. Together with your partner, you play a part, improvising as you go along, guided by the dream's symbols and emotions. This technique allows you to locate any tensions that may otherwise stay hidden in your unconscious, and bring them out into the open where you can try to resolve them.

Role play can be done at any time, but the evening is best – not least because it offers the most hopeful prospects of further dreams being stimulated by your "production." Of course, you will need to make notes on your dream in the morning, as preparation.

The dreamer starts by narrating the whole dream in as much detail as possible – this is the equivalent of actors giving a play its "read-through." Then choose your parts. The most obvious approach to casting is for the dreamer to play themselves, and the listener to play the most significant figure. Remember, this is an improvisation, so that you need have no worries about elaborating beyond the requirements of the basic dreamscript – indeed it is the departures from the script that are most revealing. After the first performance, you might try reversing the roles. Or the listener, instead of playing a human character, might choose to play the part of an animal or even an inanimate object. For example, as a telephone they might ring unexpectedly with a message from the unconscious, or from a character who is indirectly involved in the dream but not actually present. The only limits are the limits imposed by your own imagination.

EXERCISE 13

Shooing the Monsters

Dream role play can be a potent method for dealing with anxiety dreams — whether the anxieties arise from aspects of your relationship, or from external factors.

I. If you have had an anxiety dream, which you wish to explore, play yourself as the victim. First, describe the dream and the feelings it invoked. Your partner chooses a part that is calculated to provide a defense or counter-attack against the most destructive element in the dream. For example, if the dream featured a grizzly bear that came out of the woods to threaten your tent, your partner might play a mounted policeman, a gladiator with a huge net, or a bee to distract and outwit the lumbering mammal.

2. Now the role play begins. Its success depends on your partner's imagination convincing you, through imagery and narrative, that you no longer have anything to fear. You, as the victim, can ask "what if?" questions, and the non-dreamer must try to foil them — through mime, sound effects, and dialogue. For example, if you ask, "What if the bear is angered by my bearskin hat?" your partner, as a gladiator, might reply that they will lend you their helmet instead.

3. By turning anxiety into entertainment, with strong overtones of the ridiculous, you defuse the bad feelings. If the same images occur again in your dreams, they might well be the cause of bemusement rather than dread.

The Light of Reason

Dreamwork, being a window into the unconscious mind, offers access to a rich source of personal insight, but to act solely on the message from a dream is as short-sighted as ignoring it. Our various states of consciousness are designed to enhance each other: the emotional depth of dream life needs complementing with the rationality and common sense of waking consciousness. Our unconscious is the knowledge that lies within us, and reason is the tool with which we can prize it out and transform it into the inner wisdom upon which we act.

But it is not easy to use waking reason to build on the insights given to us by our dreams, especially if the dream messages seem to conflict with what waking logic tells us, or if our dream counsel is at odds with what our partner or our friends are saying. It can take courage to accept that dream emotions are truthful and revealing, and tend to be more reliable than our conscious feelings.

While it is certain that we will discover both positive and negative aspects of ourselves in our dreams, what happens if we do not like what we find? How do we react if, for example, our dreams feel consistently angry, when we have always regarded ourselves as a calm person? Bear in mind that your view of your own personality may be distorted: perhaps your dreams are nudging you toward a useful self-insight?

Beware of using dreams to rationalize situations in your own favor. To avoid this, try to use the waking mind as an intuitive, imaginative friend rather than as the person who does the tidying up, neatly putting things away in boxes to avoid a mess. The aim is to follow all the loose ends and play them out to their conclusions, not

Seeing Eye to Eye

On any given issue, the messages of your dreaming mind may find themselves at odds with those of your partner's unconscious. If you both translate your own messages into waking life, you may find that resentment builds up, as you each listen to your unconscious and hear different things.

Mutual dreamwork involves integrating the lessons of your own and your partner's dreams into a single, coherent analysis. Working on one specific issue at a time, present your dreams to each other for scrutiny — try not to assume that your dreams are more meaningful than theirs, or vice versa. Then, weave the dreams together as if they were a single narrative — how can they be interwoven and made to complement one another? Record the dreams and the narratives in a journal (see p. 77), so that you have a log of how you worked through various issues, and learned to compromise on them.

to tie them all together in a perfect bow. It is during this reasoning process that our partner's or friends' opinions can be of immense value. We need to ask for their perspective, especially when we find that a particularly uncharacteristic or disturbing dream emotion predominates. While we may be convinced that the sunken ship, the ransacked house, and every other symbol of destruction in our dreams refers to an ongoing conflict with our in-laws, our partner can point out that the dreams may refer to something else entirely, and that perhaps our interpretation is a way to justify and reinforce the feelings we have toward our relatives.

Rationalizing through discussion is bound to turn up some differences of opinion. If startling things are said, do not worry — whatever perspectives arise are merely the result of your dreams' license to misbehave.

Fighting Demons

There is no such thing as a trouble-free relationship. The difficulties you experience together may be internal — that is, arising from emotional needs that cannot be reconciled without compromise. However, shared external factors will also inevitably come into play, perhaps aggravating or throwing into focus some of the differences in temperament that a couple may have to contend with. Money is a recurrent bugbear, as are the conflicting requirements of work and domestic life. Dreams of relationship turmoil may in fact be fuelled largely by such factors — even though there will usually be an emotional component too. Look out for clues in your dreams to the nature of these issues, and try to tackle them in waking life through pragmatic and constructive decision-making together.

Sheila and Tom had a happy relationship until, without any apparent reason, they started becoming irritable with each other. Then one night Tom dreamed of coconut trees swaying in the breeze, and of Sheila climbing up one of the trees like a monkey. Although he feared a negative response from his partner, he plucked up the courage to tell her his dream, and together they tried to probe how it might relate to their relationship, in the past or present. It was Tom who remembered an occasion when Sheila had complained to him about the air pollution in the street outside their apartment. Further discussion revealed that Sheila had resented Tom's making light of her grievance, and this was the underlying cause of their relationship dissatisfaction. The monkey, they decided, was a mischievous irrelevance, and their laughter over this amusing comparison helped to seal their reconciliation.

EXERCISE 14

Shrinking the Dragon

Sometimes we are unable to deal effectively with a problem because it has no easily graspable form. The following visualization turns money worries into a conquerable dragon. You can adapt the imagery for any problem: for example, if your father-in-law interferes in your lives, visualize dousing the dragon's fiery breath with water.

1. Hold hands with your partner, breathing deeply until you both feel calm.

2. Visualize your money worries as a fire-breathing dragon – the scales on its back are gold coins. Each of you should describe the dragon in turn until you both see the same image clearly in your mind's eye.

3. Now imagine that you hold a huge sword. Visualize your partner running behind the dragon, forcing it to turn round and make itself dizzy. As it turns, you jab its scaly back with your sword, knocking off some of the coins. Gradually, the dragon shrinks in size.

4. Each of you spends five minutes on the visualization, with a final image of the dragon as nothing more than a small lizard. Visualize picking up the reptile and passing it between you. This animal can be controlled and tamed – just as your money worries can be overcome.

5. Before sleep, repeat together the affirmation that you will overcome any pecuniary problems. As you fall asleep, think of how you passed the lizard back and forth between you in your visualization. Your dreams may offer guidance on how the lizard, the manageable symbol of your concerns, may be tamed – after all money is not everything!

Keeping in Touch

Sometimes even effective communication with our partner on important issues seems in some way unsatisfactory, as if the whole point of the relationship is being missed. One problem with focusing on mutual issues is that the tone of the dialogue can become somber. When the serious conversation comes to an end, there is often a residue of anxiety that is hard to shake off. It seems trivial to ignore the problems you have been discussing, yet you have reached a point at which to go over your dilemmas yet again seems counterproductive. You may then begin to drift apart a little emotionally, becoming stiff and awkward with each other.

Dreamwork as a means of keeping in touch offers a useful middle ground between the serious and playful. There are only so many arguments that reason can bring to bear. Dreamwork broadens the vocabulary of debate and increases the likelihood of imaginative and unorthodox solutions. At the same time, there can be an element of lightheartedness about it even when serious questions are being addressed. This can improve waking conversation by providing a safety valve, a way of letting go.

The one place where major difficulties in a relationship (such as conflicting needs, money problems, the allocation of responsibilities, and so on) should not normally be discussed is the bedroom. Try to keep this as a special setting where, if you address important themes at all, it is through some form of dreamwork. Remember that dreaming is a useful tool to keep effective communication open when it is problematic at a more explicit level. In the bedroom agree to give the unconscious more authority than the conscious mind and the power of reason.

EXERCISE 15

The Dream Connection

How can we connect with someone when our opinions are far apart, or when hurt feelings prevent true contact in waking reality? This exercise demonstrates the power of dream telepathy, and shows how reaching out to a loved one or a friend in their dreams can deliver your message.

1. At bedtime, lie still, breathing regularly. Clear your mind of mental chatter.

2. When you feel relaxed, visualize yourself floating against a calming, blue background. Imagine yourself at peace yet invigorated by a beautiful white light that emanates from within, bathing you in its radiant aura. Feel the warmth and serenity that the light brings to you.

3. Next, visualize your partner or friend floating next to you. Imagine that you have asked them to join you and try to sense their presence. They are also at peace and surrounded by light.

4. When the image has become stable, imagine that you move slowly closer together until the two auras coalesce into one.

5. Now "think" your message to this person. It should be short, loving, and non-judgmental. It may, for example, express a desire to get in contact or offer a conciliatory apology.

6. You can now drift off to sleep. You may not experience a dream related to this telepathy exercise, but the person you are seeking to reach may find a symbol in their dreams that carries your message.

Releasing Resentment

Dreamwork can offer an antidote to resentment, which often creeps insidiously into relationships. Resentment stores up grievances, each building on the one before until we no longer recognize our partner as the person we love. Instead we see only their faults, often magnified out of all proportion. If we tune in to our dreams together, we can release such resentment before it reaches crisis level.

One characteristic of resentments is that they are usually unreasonable. For example, we might be annoyed by our partner's perpetual optimism in the face of day-to-day difficulties, whereas the real problem could well be our own pessimism. If, in our dreams, our partner behaves in ways that increase our feelings of resentment, we can use dreamwork to help us understand the situation from perspectives other than our own. Let us say that, in a dream, the optimist (your partner) walks into a lion's cage without any means of self-protection, and you are left standing on the outside feeling fearful for their safety and annoyed by their recklessness. When you come to analyze this dream together, your partner might confess that their apparent disregard for safety was in fact bravado — they were afraid inside but acted bravely to demonstrate their love and commitment.

A variation on this theme is to agree that when the dreamer describes their dream they will recount the actions and symbols accurately, but lie about some feelings. The listener has to guess which feelings were false and work out what was *really* felt. The idea is to get the listener to identify more closely with the dreamer's point of view. If your resentments are to be brought to the surface, it is better that your partner guesses them than that you have to make your own statement of complaint.

EXERCISE 16

Up and Away

This is an exercise to do as you drift off to sleep, when you are in the hypnagogic *(between waking and sleeping) state. Its purpose is to resolve, in a lighthearted way, any niggling resentments or irritations that have occurred between you and your partner during the day, and to glide you into pleasant, trouble-free dreams.*

1. Lying in bed, each partner in turn describes their irritations during the day in a gently comic way. (It is agreed that the bedroom is a resentment-free zone where even serious issues become lighter.) The object is to cause amusement, and turn the irritations into a set of harmless images.

2. Next, one of you describes, in a quiet voice, the many tiny soapbubbles rising out of your minds toward the ceiling. Then, each soapbubble containing one of the comic images you have found for your resentments, floats slowly upward and bursts on the ceiling.

3. The speaker begins to talk more and more dreamily about the bubbles, as they waft upward. The aim is to soften the mood so that you can both relax gently into sleep: for example, you might describe the lightness and ethereal beauty of the bubbles.

4. So enjoyable is this pre-sleep scenario that you are both reluctant to relinquish it for actual sleep. But as you finally let yourselves drift off, you can reflect that your thoughts have been thoroughly cleansed of all petty resentments, and you can look forward together to your dreams. Nothing could be more natural.

Liberating Desires

The ancient Greeks believed that dreams about sex were signs of an infected mind: they were thought to be inspired by demons that corrupt our brains with evil desires. In the 1950's American researcher Dr Alfred Kinsey claimed that most adults have sexual dreams – a statement that caused a storm of controversy. Today, we have moved far from the mythic beliefs of the Greeks, and no longer tend to be affronted by Kinsey's findings, but even so, many of us dislike admitting to sexual dreams and find sex a difficult subject for discussion.

In fact, erotic dreams offer a unique way to ignite our sex lives, liberate desires, overcome inhibitions, and enhance intimacy. In telling your partner about your sexual dreams you establish a mood of sensuality, and communicate desire, and this is a simple yet effective way to rekindle passion. The novel and unpredictable erotic images that may appear in a sexual dream often trigger dormant feelings of excitement in both of you that can inject new zest into your sex life.

You may find the eroticism you or your partner experience in your dream life powerfully stimulating, even if it features the unusual or bizarre. Try not to read any deep message into this: there is nothing to fear from feeling excited by a dream that depicts you doing something far more daring than you would normally do when awake. Remember, it does not mean you have a hidden desire to act out what you have dreamed, but it reflects the erotic impulses from the *id*, the part of our unconscious in which our basic libidinous needs are generated.

Sexual excitement often springs from unusual situations – the very unlikelihood of having satisfactory sex in particular circumstances leads to

EXERCISE 17

The Beaufort Scale of Dream Sex

Wind speed is conventionally measured according to the Beaufort Scale, which ranges from 0 (when smoke from a chimney goes straight up) to 12 and upward (when hurricanes rip the roofs from houses). It is fun to measure your dreams against the following Beaufort Scale of eroticism, and to discuss the score of a particular dream with your partner.

0 Anxiety dreams in which the symbols seem non-sexual — for example, dreams of pennilessness or speaking in public.

1 Dreams reflecting emotional problems, such as claustrophobia or drowning.

2 Pleasant dreams of softness — perhaps featuring silky textures, smooth peaches, or the softness of flower petals.

3 Pleasant dreams of the sensation of touch, such as massage or hair brushing.

4 Exciting dreams featuring the elements — for example, strong winds or volcanic eruptions.

5 Dreams of settings associated with intimacy — the bedroom or dressing room; objects such as mirrors, pillows, and underwear.

6 Arousing dreams of nudity or partial nudity, such as the fleeting glimpse of a naked body through an open window.

7 Fulfilling sexual encounters, which may feature your current or previous partner, a friend, an acquaintance, or even a stranger.

As you work out your dream scores with your partner, you might find that you become more sensitive to sexual nuances and that, as you discuss these matters, your sex life gathers momentum.

arousal. We are all familiar with the desire that is increased by obstacles that lie in the way of its satisfaction — the urge to make love while we are in a restaurant or at the theater, or the desire that comes over us during a long-distance phone call.

This syndrome can be used to good effect in dream conversations. If we lie in bed with our partner and talk over dreams whose content is sexually neutral, but we relate the dream in a sensual and erotic way, we may find desire welling up as we do so. For example, in describing the wind as it caresses the leaves of a tree, you might find that your metaphor of caressing turns into reality. When reporting a dream, concentrate on aspects of touch, textures, and close detail. A good principle when sharing dreams in the morning is to incorporate metaphors of the body. Do not do so with the conscious intention of stimulating arousal, but do not be surprised if arousal is the result!

Dreams can sometimes help to liberate us from a block by making us more aware of its underlying causes. For example, one of the most common dreams of inhibition is a lovemaking session interrupted by some outside agency — perhaps an authority figure (such as your father, a priest, or a teacher), or some inanimate cause (the alarm clock going off or the bed collapsing). Look carefully at the agent of interruption to see if it contains any elements symbolizing aspects of yourself. Perhaps the father is your own sense of responsibility toward your children, rather than your real father? Perhaps the alarm clock reflects a strongly-held work ethic that equates sensuality with self-indulgence? By testing and probing in this way, and above all working through the dream with your partner, you may throw light on some of the difficulties that burden your intimate moments.

EXERCISE 18

Scents and Desires

Scents trigger intense emotional reactions, and are potent dream incubators. Sensual aromas can direct sexual energy into our dream life. This exercise shows how, by exploring the effects of different scents on your levels of desire, you can try to increase the frequency and vividness of erotic dreams.

1. Sit down with your lover and each of you make a list of your own favorite smells. These could be anything — do not forget the obvious ones, such as freshly ground coffee, newly-mown grass, or citrus fruits. Which of the fragrances on your list do you most associate with sensual pleasure and eroticism?

2. Compare lists. Begin your experiments with those erotic scents on which you both agree (you need not both have written down the same scents to agree on them — it might be that your partner thought of one that you had not). As long as the scent is pleasurable to you both, and easy to reproduce in the bedroom, the experiment will be conducted in the best conditions.

3. Seek out the scents. Perhaps they are available as essential oils for use on an aromatherapy burner (most are nowadays). With such items as coffee you could fall asleep with a steaming, fresh cup by your bedside.

4. Drift off to sleep with the scent filling the room. (You may even like to try a pre-sleep massage with a massage oil of the same or another erotic scent: gently rub the oil into your partner's back, making long sweeping movements with your hands over their skin.) When you wake up in the morning, compare your dreams. Did the scent work? Keep experimenting and comparing your dreams until you have both found your perfect erotic scent.

The Virtual Dream Kit

*T*here may be times when we have a particular issue that we wish to discuss with our partner, but do not know how, and nothing in our dreams seems to suggest itself as a springboard into the topic. This chapter is intended to solve such an impasse by presenting a repertoire of "virtual dreams." Five commonplace relationship issues are covered. Each has a brief description on the way in which that issue might appear in actual dreams. Then, alongside, follows a virtual dream on the topic in question — a dream-like scenario, rich in symbolism. Instead of actually having a dream, you can use this given scenario as a starting-point for dreamwork with a partner — just as you might if the dream had been real. We have given some guidelines on identifying the symbols, as well as interpretation cues for you to work with. If you wish, you can fill out the story by extending the narrative.

Of course, there is nothing to prevent you from incubating the scenario before bedtime to see if your unconscious commandeers the virtual dream to make an actual appearance as you sleep.

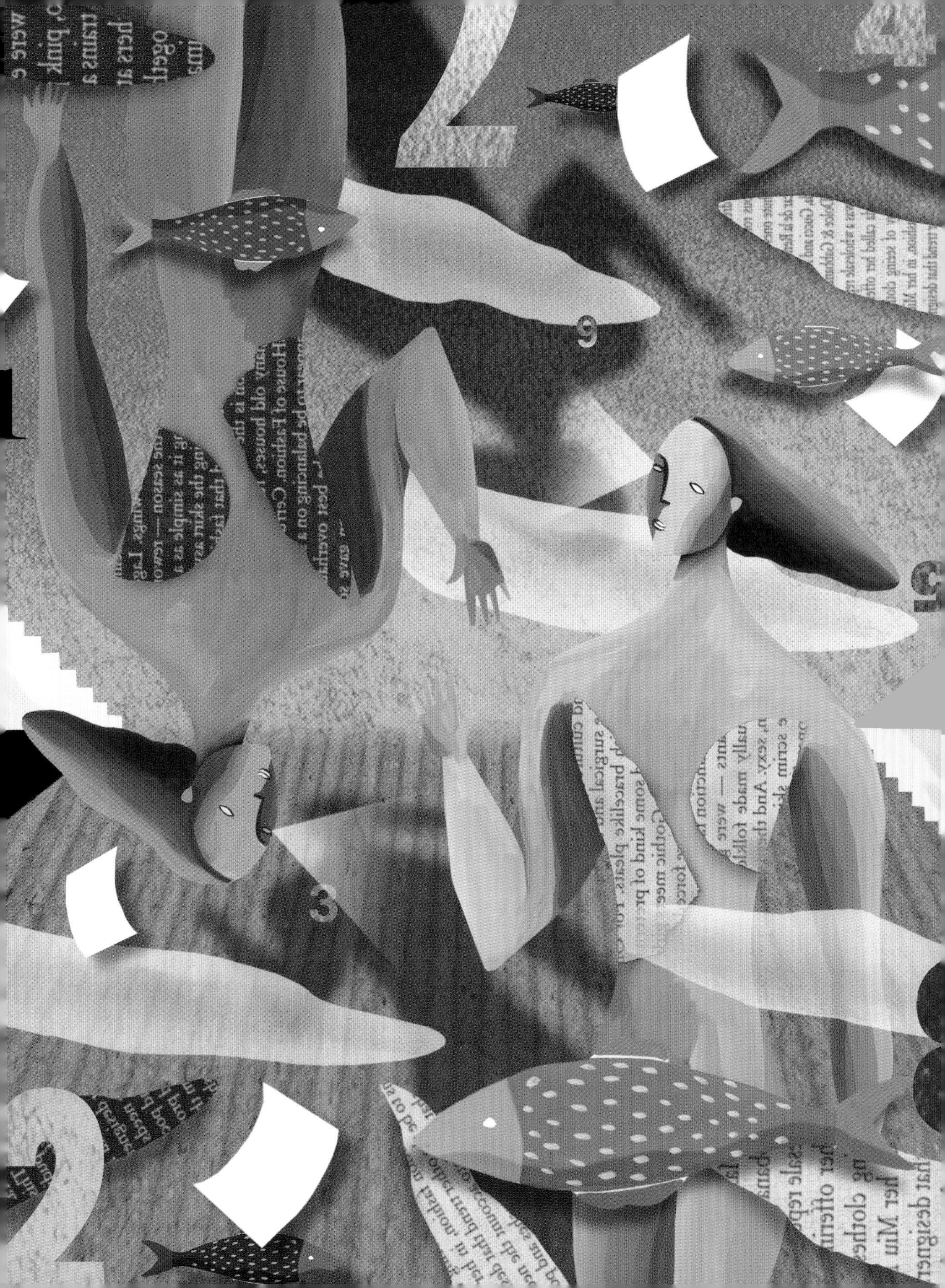

Love Triangles

Although we are not always willing to admit it, there comes a time in every relationship when we find ourselves attracted, perhaps even tempted, by someone else. Of course, acting on this impulse causes a world of trouble that may damage your relationship irreparably, but sometimes the thoughts and feelings alone are enough to breed guilt and hurt — even fantasies can bring with them the specter of broken trust. To make matters worse, this is the one issue that most couples find almost impossible to talk about.

When you are held hostage by feelings for someone other than your partner, expect your dreams to reflect your state of mind, and to feel insecure or guilt-ridden. Dream emotions will take precedence over what may be a barrage of turbulent symbolism. You may dream of exposure or hiding, of broken objects, or of scenarios involving lack of trust. As your waking consciousness moves toward giving in to your feelings or worrying obsessively about them, your dreams will echo these emotions with a similar intensity.

One problem with love triangles is that both alternatives can seem equally undesirable. On the one hand, we feel unable to resist temptation, on the other we fear the consequences of breaking up an established relationship — or of being found out if we unwisely attempt double-dealing. It can be useful to ask your dreams for guidance in such a situation. Try repeating a question such as "How do I really feel about my relationship?" before you go to sleep. Once your dreams help you to discover where your heart truly lies, you can face your emotional dilemma in waking life with new strength.

A Ship on Stormy Seas

The Virtual Dream

A sailing ship enters turbulent waters and is tossed about on the waves so roughly that it is in danger of sinking. The crew are terrified by the ferocity of the storm and look to the captain to save them from this life-threatening ordeal. But the captain dithers — he has never faced such a dramatic situation before, and he is unsure what to do for the best. Fearful and guilt-ridden, he hides away in his quarters as the crew bang at the door, begging for direction and a plan that will save their lives.

The Symbols

The sea was considered by Jung to be an image of the unconscious and it is also a Freudian symbol of sexual union. Its turbulence may refer to tensions within your permanent relationship, to the passion you feel for someone else, or to the guilt this passion has stirred in you. The floundering ship may symbolize your established relationship, while the crew could represent either an internal element (your conscience) or an external element (pressure from other people).

The Cues

What does this storm feel like to you? Is it exciting or frightening or a mixture of both? Why do you, as captain, feel so alone? Why do you feel so incapable of making a decision? Do you really believe that the ship will sink if you do not act decisively? Do you have a strong sense of impending danger? Do you feel safer in your cabin than on deck? If so, why? If you were a crew member, what would you be shouting? Should you take evasive action or ride out the storm? Are there lifeboats on board? If so, do they function and are you able to reach them? If the crew were to abandon ship, would you follow? If so, how would this make you feel? If you were to stay on board, alone, how would you feel then?

Losing and Finding

Our emotional lives are often described in terms of a quest — we search for the right partner, for love and fulfillment. Conversely, we might speak of losing someone close to us, or losing love itself. It is hardly surprising, then, that our dreams use imagery of discovery and loss, often in a literal sense, to mirror the highs and lows of our emotional experiences.

Treasures such as diamonds, rings, gold coins, and other precious items constitute a glittering repertoire of symbols that denote value. When interpreting dreams about love and relationships the difficulty lies in deciding where this value resides. If we dream of a jewel, could this be the loved one in disguise, the person whose scintillating qualities we have recognized and commandeered to bring light into our own lives? Or is the meaning something more abstract, a metaphor for truth, virtue, or constancy? As always in dreamwork, we need to find a way of judging between conflicting readings. By interpreting the jewel literally as a gemstone, or as a symbol of material wealth, we could perhaps have missed another, more important meaning.

We should not assume automatically that a precious object in a dream measures high on the scale against which the waking mind measures its assets — the unconscious mind, wise old magus that it is, often recognizes that the true value lies elsewhere. Similarly, profound loss in a dream, perhaps even the loss of life itself, can sometimes signify a relatively trivial separation or a minor misfortune, even though such images can haunt the waking mind for some time afterward.

The Vase and the Dove

The Virtual Dream

A man and a woman are arguing. The man wants to spend a month traveling alone — a long-held ambition. As they argue, the man backs into a table, whereupon a precious Chinese vase — an heirloom belonging to the woman — falls to the floor and shatters. The couple break off arguing when they notice a roundish object on the floor, rolling away from the shattered pieces of the vase. The man bends down to pick it up. It is an egg. As he holds it, the egg hatches, and a tiny dove emerges, fanning out its tail as it nestles in the palm of his hand.

The Symbols

The precious Chinese vase could represent the couple's relationship, which will suffer if the man goes traveling, but because he finds an egg, which in turn hatches into the dove, there are indications that the outcome will be positive. If there are prospects of having a child, perhaps the egg refers to offspring. Or the dove (a symbol of peace) could refer to restored harmony, the patching up of quarrels. But in the biblical Flood story the dove flew back, usefully, with evidence of land — should the man travel after all?

The Cues

If you had this dream, what might the vase represent? How would you feel when the vase broke? Why would you have been quarreling? What would be your reaction when you first see the egg? And what might the egg represent? Could there be any connection between the breaking of the vase and the egg discovered inside it? Could it be that traveling is a metaphor for some other ambition? What do you think is the significance of the dove? How do you feel when you first see it? Why is it so small? Is it strong enough to fly? Where will it fly to when it takes wing?

Voices

Communication is unquestionably the single most important element in a relationship. Couples who communicate well are able to surmount even the greatest obstacles, while those who cannot connect can be hampered by the simplest problems. But even in healthy relationships, communication is not easy. It requires constant attention and nurturing to avoid misunderstandings, erroneous mind reading, jumping to conclusions, and plainly not listening to what your partner is trying to say.

When voices, or other obvious forms of dialogue, occur in a dream, interpretation is usually relatively easy. For example, if you dream of deafness, blindness, or language barriers — all types of impaired communication — you may be avoiding talking or otherwise expressing your feelings to your partner. Or perhaps you feel that they are ignoring your feelings. In either scenario, the solution is to find a sensitive way to reopen communication channels between you.

Dreams of methods of communication such as telephones, letters, e-mail, and so on are common, and may reflect the importance to you of particular devices in waking life. They indicate that there are problems with communication in your relationship, but in order to find out their cause you need to probe deeper into the content and context of each dream. Symbols such as someone shouting or screaming at you, or engaging in loud-mouthed behavior in your presence, are also commonplace, and often mean, quite literally, that you are not hearing what your partner is trying to say to you. You can expect the voices in these dreams to grow louder until you acknowledge whatever you have been missing or avoiding.

Gibberish, Gestures, and Drawings in the Sand

The Virtual Dream

You find yourself on an exotic desert island. At first you think you are alone but then you discover that there is another presence — a total stranger whose language and methods of communication are completely foreign. The stranger tries desperately to communicate something to you, talking loudly and frantically, but you fail to understand a word that they are saying, as their language seems based on a structure entirely different from your own. The figure gesticulates, draws in the sand, and uses physical movement, but all to no avail.

The Symbols

Desert islands often signify isolation, while unsuccessful attempts to conduct a dialogue obviously symbolize a breakdown in communication. Consider who the stranger might represent: could they be an archetypal figure, such as the Trickster (a mischievous saboteur whose energies can serve as a corrective) or the Shadow (the dark side of the ego)? Could they be the Wise Old Man or Woman (the accumulated wisdom of humanity and the knowledge to which we aspire)? Or is the stranger simply a straightforward representation of your partner?

The Cues

Are you an inhabitant of the island or a castaway? Do you feel safe here? Is the stranger a friendly figure or a potential threat? Is the figure ambiguous? What are the characteristics of the figure's language? Is this language more or less expressive than your own? Are the syllables distinct or muffled? Why do you think the stranger is so frantic to communicate with you? Why do you find it so difficult to understand the stranger's sign language? What symbols does the figure draw in the sand? If you had to make a guess at the message the stranger is trying to convey, what would it be?

Parting and Reunion

It is only in certain exceptional relationships that couples do not experience at least short periods apart. It is said that Paul and Linda McCartney never spent a single night away from each other in their 29 years of marriage; if true, this is a miraculous achievement. The reality for most couples is that one partner needs to spend time away from home occasionally, perhaps for work or family matters, or to pursue independent leisure pursuits.

In today's psychological climate, in which we are supposed to be whole within ourselves, it is not fashionable to admit to anxiety: a partner is almost an emotional luxury. Yet, far more couples than one might realize struggle silently to cope with separations, particularly if they are long or unpredictable. At such times, dreams convey what we truly feel — they are not constricted by the social conventions that put pressure on us to ignore our inner disquiet.

A parting in a dream can indicate the need to move on to a new phase in your life. If it is you, the dreamer, who is embarking on a journey, it may be that you are at a transitional point in your relationship, but not necessarily ready to move away — perhaps you are looking for deeper commitment. Parting dreams can also reflect an urge to spend some time developing your own potential.

We can sometimes have a dream of reunion as a *dream of compensation*, an attempt by our unconscious to make us feel better about a difficult situation in waking life. But, equally, dreams of reunion could be a sign that your relationship is now strong and healthy once more, even if you are not consciously aware of this.

The Departing Train

The Virtual Dream

You are at a train station with your lover, who is leaving on a trip. You kiss them goodbye and watch as they turn and disappear into the crowd that is climbing aboard the train. You wave to each other as the train slowly pulls out of the station. You are left standing alone on the platform, while the general hubbub of the station carries on around you. You make your way back to the station entrance to leave, and find that there is a group of people there, waiting for you. One of them is holding up a signboard with lettering on it.

The Symbols

A train is a male sexual symbol according to Freud, but it also represents freedom from responsibility. Your lover departing on a trip by train could symbolize your feeling that they are running away from their commitments. It also suggests a temporary separation — which need not necessarily be physical. The group of people waiting for you at the station entrance could reflect the fact that you are not really alone, as you have a good support structure of friends and family around you; or it could imply that there are other people who are attracted to you, waiting to take your partner's place. The sign with the lettering could convey a special message, or it might be a way to attract your attention, or to denote that you have been singled out in some way.

The Cues

How do you feel as you kiss your lover goodbye at the station? Where are they going? How long will they be away? What are your thoughts as their train pulls out of the station? How do you feel now that you are alone on the platform? Who are the people waiting for you at the station entrance? Are they friendly or hostile? Are you surprised to see them or did you expect them to be there? Who is the person holding up the signboard? What does the lettering say? How do you feel when you realize the significance of the signboard?

Past and Present

For reasons that can be hard to fathom, some relationships seem cursed by time. The joys of the present somehow seem to be blighted by what has happened in the past. Often the problem is that the shadow of a former love has fallen over our relationship. Events that unfolded long before we met our partner exert a spectral influence — sometimes making the relationship seem triangular. How do we expel this interloper from our lives, and start to breathe a purer air?

When we feel the presence of our partner's former lover within our relationship, it is difficult to feel secure. We are trapped into comparing ourselves with our ghostly rival, and also comparing the quality of our partner's love. When this happens, the cause is often our own insecurity. We may even ask about the old flame, which serves only to make matters worse.

Dreams of possessiveness and hoarding may reflect this retrospective jealousy. For example, we might dream of keeping our partner captive at home, possibly even tied up. Alternatively, we might dream of our partner being out of reach — perhaps on the other side of a chasm, or in a different building, glimpsed only through a window.

Dreaming of a figure who represents a threat to your happiness should not be taken in itself as confirmation of your fears. Perhaps the dream is suggesting that this person can play a perfectly harmless role in your life. If he or she seems to be getting closer, this could be interpreted as a gesture of reassurance or welcome. If the dream's mood is hostile, ask yourself whether anything in the setting or action contradicts this feeling.

The Clever Pupil

The Virtual Dream

You are at school again, sitting in your old classroom, facing the teacher. On display all around the classroom are the best pupil's personal projects. Someone in front of you is answering all the teacher's questions. When you are asked for an answer, your mind goes blank and you burst into tears. You decide to leave the class, and you stand up. You go to pick up your schoolbag, but as you lift it, it feels enormously heavy. The dream ends abruptly as you struggle with the load.

The Symbols

The teacher may be a representation of the archetypal Wise Old Man or Woman, who stands for both the accumulated wisdom of humanity and the higher knowledge to which we aspire, or the Hero — the awakened inner self that aspires to inner growth and quests for true understanding. Or the teacher may be a simple depiction of your partner. The display of the best pupil's projects could refer to your partner's former lover, while picking up the schoolbag may hint at a challenge that you need to face.

The Cues

What subject are you being taught? What does the teacher think of you? Do you like the clever pupil? If so, why? What do you admire about them? If you do not like them, why not? Does the clever pupil get poor marks for some subjects? Do you get better marks than them in any subjects? If so, in which ones? How do you feel when the teacher praises them? What would happen if the clever pupil made a mistake? What would you do if they sought you out as a special friend? What might the teacher have asked you? Why could you not answer? Why do you wish to leave the class? What is inside your schoolbag to make it so heavy?

Friends, Family, and Foes

Naturally, any relationship that is important in our waking life, whether with a family member, a friend, a colleague, an adversary, or even a marginal acquaintance, may be represented in our dreams.

This chapter explores how these relationships appear in our dream life and the different concerns that each type of relationship raises. We discover the nature of family symbolism, and how this may have reflected our psychological development since childhood. We examine how dreaming of friends emphasizes our need to connect deeply with others and reminds us that secure and comfortable friendships, although we often taken them for granted, are rare and wonderful, and to be cherished. When we duel with a professional or personal adversary, dreaming reveals our true feelings and motivation, and also guides us as to how best to approach and interact with even the most difficult person. Dreams of mere acquaintances may indicate that we have a greater connection with them, or what they represent, than we consciously realize.

Friendships

We are rarely surprised when we meet friends in dreams. Sometimes they appear exactly as they do in waking life, sometimes they are altered in some way, or they appear in strange guises, or say things that are uncharacteristic of them. We may dream of friendships in the present or, equally, from the past, as our unconscious mind never forgets anyone, and it is not unusual for a particular friend to make repeated appearances — even if we lost contact with them a long time ago.

There are differences in the way male and female dreams of friendship manifest themselves. Among women, friendships tend to be open, communicative, and physically expressive, and this can lead to dreams that are rather like conversations with a confidante. By contrast, men's dreams of friendship tend to be latent, less expressive, and sometimes enigmatic.

Often the dreaming mind treats a friendship as if it were more emotional than its waking manifestation. The value of such dreams is that they can open our minds to the importance of a particular friend in our lives. Why not simply tell your friends about the dreams in which they appear, without any attempt at interpretation? This can provide a healthy corrective to the tendency, especially between men, for feelings to be left unrevealed. Once the dream is shared, it is as if feelings between the dreamer and the friend have been released incognito, in a way that causes no embarrassment. Yet the option of interpretation still remains open to the listener, and the recounting of the dream creates an intriguing bridge to which either party might at any time choose to return.

EXERCISE 19

Animal Magic

We tend to lean heavily on our friendships in times of emotional need. Why not invite your best friend to appear in your dreams and guide you through the dream adventures you hope to have? An effective way to do this is to identify the friend with an animal that represents one of their positive characteristics, and incubate dreams of your chosen creature.

1. Identify your friend with the animal which you feel best represents their most outstanding quality. For example, you could choose a gazelle (speed of thought or action), an owl (wisdom), or a horse (loyalty and intelligence).

2. Each night, before you drift off to sleep at bedtime, meditate on your chosen animal, mentally imbuing it with your friend's spirit.

3. Now imagine yourself entering the world of dreams with your animal companion by your side – if you have chosen a horse, perhaps you could ride it.

4. In the morning, go back over your dreams looking for associations with your animal–friend (if not the animal itself). So, if your dream companion is a gazelle, any sudden or fast movement, or graceful gesture, could be a symbol of their presence.

5. When interpreting your dream, treat any such feature, or the part of the dream in which it occurs, as a coded oracle, offering you wisdom and advice. With practice, you may come to dream of the creature directly. As a result of these dreams, you may also develop a closer bond with your friend in waking life.

The Family

Far more than simply a group of people sharing a common genetic bond, the family is the classroom in which our attitudes about relationships are formed. In the bosom of our family we learn social and communication skills, interpersonal control, and, of course, intimacy. The family makes up our entire universe during our early, most formative, years. For better or worse, we are imprinted with our own family's unique set of spoken and unspoken rules — the blueprints for our behavior throughout life.

As well as being classrooms, families are also crucibles in which strong and often complex feelings are worked through over the years, relating to the dynamics of blood ties and dependence. Childhood problems can lie dormant for decades and then suddenly erupt. Emotional and communication difficulties can recede and advance as circumstances slowly or suddenly change.

Within our families we tend to say both too little and too much. When the usual civilities weaken under the pressure of feeling, we might criticize loudly and at length; yet embarrassment might prevent us from saying "I love you" even when this is precisely what we feel. Sibling rivalry and parent-child tensions can cause difficulties that, if left unresolved, can lead to a complete breakdown in communication — in extreme cases we can even find children "divorcing" their parents, and brothers and sisters refusing to speak to each other.

When family problems beleaguer our waking lives, our dreams will occasionally return us to childhood, when throwing a ball in the backyard or drenching each other with the garden hose was the innocent symbol of family life. Such

Who's Who in Your Dreams?

A recent study of 400 dreams (200 male and 200 female) showed that, very broadly speaking, we are more likely to dream about friends or strangers than about our own family. Why could this be? Is it because we feel that family issues are less pressing in our lives than issues associated with more recent encounters? Or is it that members of our family appear more frequently in dreams than we believe or remember? Could it be, in fact, that their appearance is so common that the dreams somehow escape the notice of our waking selves? Can it be that our relatives exert an influence without being embodied as figures? Or could it be that they appear in disguise?

It is worth reminding ourselves that dreams do not depict reality – rather, they use symbols to alert us to aspects of waking life which need our attention. Thus it is not unusual in dream-life for a stranger to display the character traits of our brother, or for our partner to take on an aspect of our own personality. Nevertheless, members of our family sometimes appear as themselves, and when they do so, it is because our unconscious has chosen this method as the best way to bring a point to our attention.

PERCENTAGE OCCURRENCES OF FAMILY SYMBOLS

MALE DREAMER		FEMALE DREAMER
10%	Mother/father	10%
2%	Sister/brother	19%
–	Daughter/son	4%
8%	Partner/spouse	10%
4%	Other family member	12%
42%	Friend/stranger	33%
6%	Female/male celebrity	2%
28%	Self/no-one	10%

dreams provide a corrective reminder of nurture, play, and family harmony. However, darker dream symbols may also emerge: of violence (not uncommon in dreams about siblings), the sexual activities of parents, and of intimacies which we consider bizarre. We should not be too concerned if the limits of propriety are exceeded. The feelings that we never show must have an escape somehow, and if our dreams are disturbing, this may be a reflection of the narrowness of their outlet rather than the urgency of their content.

When working with dreams, it is important to remember that members of the family may stand in for other themes — for example, if we dream of our son or daughter becoming separated from us, this may in fact reflect our abandonment of an ideal, or the failure of some personal ambition. Conversely, our relatives might take on alternative guises: a loud-mouthed stranger, for example, could represent in a magnified way the self-important, attention-seeking side of our father's character; or, an over-friendly or nosy stranger might represent the protectiveness of our mother, or her penchant for interfering in our lives. Of course, the positive aspects of our relationships with our family will also come through in our dreams. If, for example, in waking life we feel distanced from our sister because we have not heard from her in a while, our dreams (literally or metaphorically) might reassure us that she continues to love and care about us even in her silence — we might dream that she arrives to see us unexpectedly, laden with cakes and other delicious goodies, or that a person unknown to us hands us a flower as a symbol of our sister's love.

Dreamwork within the family can be remarkably effective as a way to bring long-standing issues into the open, and move them toward a resolution. Learning to unravel the symbolism of your dreams together can

The Mother Archetype

Among Jung's Archetypes (see p.16) is the Great Mother. She is defined by the qualities of loving care, spiritual beauty, and purity (associated with the Virgin Mary). She also has a dark side: the jealous, manipulative wicked stepmother of folk tale.

Look out for the Great Mother in your dreams. She need not necessarily appear in the shape of your real mother, but could be any female figure. Analyze any encounters that your dream self has with such women — what can they tell you about your relationship with your own mother? If, for example, a blind woman appeared, you might feel that your mother is unable to accept your independence or adulthood; if you encountered a woman nursing a baby, perhaps your dream is trying to tell you that your mother still cares for and nurtures you.

help you to open your ears to, and accept as possibly valid, the views of others. Try describing a dream at the start of a family conference, to bring in fresh perspectives on the agenda, and to encourage you all to think imaginatively and creatively about any problems that you face as a unit, in waking life. If we can transport our dream-interpretation skills into discussions on real-life issues (even those as mundane as who does the weekly shopping), unconstructive family arguments may become less frequent — and perhaps even cease altogether.

You might also consider setting up a dream correspondence between family members who live apart — perhaps a system whereby a dream gets sent, like a chain letter, from person to person with interpretations and further dreams being added at each stage.

The Policeman's Wife
Case Study

The death of a parent can affect us for longer than we consciously realize, mingling confusingly with other emotional situations. This case study shows how dreamwork can help to clarify the long-term hurts that bereavement inflicts.

Mary was the newly married wife of a police officer, who broke her vow that she would never fall in love with a cop. She knew all too well the dangers of her husband's job, because her father, a police officer for 30 years, was killed in the line of duty. But love for Jay finally triumphed over Mary's reservations. Unfortunately, her anxiety returned early on in their married life, to the extent that she began to experience periods of panic – she feared that her husband, like her father, would one day not return from work.

Her first dreams were violent and ugly – her husband was always trapped in the same, filthy, run-down house with no means of escape. He was hopelessly outnumbered by criminals, who surrounded and shot him.

Jay was sympathetic to her fears, supportively listening to her as she recounted her dreams, and assuring her that such a situation would never happen. Yet the dreams persisted, at times nightly. Mary decided to try dreamwork to cope with her fears. She wanted to find out whether they represented a legitimate concern for her husband's safety or unresolved emotions still aroused by her father's death. She also aspired to control the outcome of her dreams — could she modify their endings so that the police officer would survive?

She started to put the crucial question to her unconscious. She said to herself quietly as she drifted off to sleep, "Show me the truth of my emotions." She also thought about her father, with a view to jolting her dreams out of their predictable track.

After experimenting, Mary's dreams began to change — their images fused, sometimes representing her husband, sometimes her father. The mood of her dreams also began to shift: the police officer was still killed, yet there was a sense that maybe there was a way for him to escape from the house of death.

With more dreamwork, Mary's dreams changed further over several months. She began to dream that the police officer was wearing a protective vest that repelled his assailants' bullets, and he could now shoot back and scare off the would-be murderers, then escape through a trapdoor in the floor.

Over time, Mary's recurrent dreams of death became less frequent, and when they did occur the outcome was more positive. She was able gradually to accept her husband's occupation, and also found herself grieving and coping better with her father's death. While she still needed Jay's constant support and reassurance, her panic episodes slowly disappeared and her anxiety became far less disabling.

In the Workplace

The workplace spawns some of our most challenging relationships. It is the one place outside the family where we are obliged to interact closely with others, through circumstance, not choice. The inevitable conflicts that emerge at work are often dismissed as office politics, which is small comfort, as we must still find a way to get along with our colleagues and work effectively with them, for eight hours most days, year in, year out.

The inherent competitiveness of the workplace (most obviously expressed in the promotion race) is readily translated into dream terms. The more ambitious we are, the more likely we are to dream of the people whom we perceive to be jockeying for position. At such times, our dreams will probably feature symbols of struggle, and have a combative urgency that is reminiscent of childhood battles with brothers or sisters. Resentment is also a common theme in workplace dreams, especially if we fail to receive our expected rewards. Then, our only recourse may be to express our frustration through dream retribution, which is healthier than bottling up such emotions, or acting them out in waking life. Competitive jealousy may also be awakened in a dream but we might be tempted to interpret this emotion in the light of our love life, rather than our working life — a mistake that can wreak havoc in a partnership if it is not soon corrected.

The relationships that we have with our superiors present a tricky challenge. These interactions are a mixture of parent-child and peer dynamics and, while we may develop a friendship with our boss, it is governed by a uniquely complex

The Damsel in Armor

Sexual harassment at work can be subtle and hard to deal with, but by harnessing your dream power, it is possible to defend yourself without resorting to making a formal complaint against anyone.

Begin by incubating dreams to rid yourself of your pest — one worker dreamed of a glistening liquid that seeped out of her pores, to cover and protect her, as well as repel her would-be assailant.

Try to stimulate dreams of strength and personal protection. The confidence your dreams give you can then help you to project an aura to rebuff the offender, so that they will no longer find you as desirable as before. Although this may sound a poor defense, sexual harassment is often more to do with playing psychological power games than it is to do with sexual desire.

set of rules. Dreams can offer us an insight into the true dynamics of such a relationship by cutting through the maze of protocol, so that we become aware of what is really going on.

The workplace is a cultural environment that normally does not lend itself to any discussion of dreams or other references to the world of the unconscious: sales targets, critical-path analysis, and performance-linked bonuses do not sit well with revelations of vulnerability. However, it can be effective and salutary to refer to a dream now and then in unexpected circumstances — for example, at a team meeting. Such a ploy, if not introduced in an inappropriate way, can add a new creative dimension to a discussion, and this in turn could encourage the workforce to think in more imaginative and productive ways.

Dreaming of the Enemy

It would be unrealistic to imagine that we live among people who are, without exception, wholly benevolent to us. Daily interactions mean that from time to time we will, almost inevitably, encounter others whose personality, mood, or manner jars with our own, to leave us feeling as if we have been treated badly or have ourselves behaved in an unfriendly way. But harboring resentment achieves nothing, and we need to find a way to re-open contact with the estranged party.

How do we learn, through our dreams, to extend the hand of peace and heal wounds in our long-term relationships and beyond, to turn enemies into friends and hostile encounters into fulfilling ones? Our dreams, always the bearers of the truth, warn us when we are being unreasonable, or when others are behaving unreasonably toward us. But, instead of simply recognizing dream warnings, it is preferable to let them become an impetus for release. Think of such dreams as comedies, mimicking and mocking the ridiculous nature of petty disputes, and the anger they generate. Even if a particular dream seemed to contain only serious elements, try to imagine it as a comedy – imagine roars of laughter from an unseen audience. Not only will this process help you assess the reality of the situation with kindlier eyes, it will also encourage you to stay more detached from its negative emotions, and hasten the resolution of the conflict.

Another technique is to imagine yourself stepping into your dream to act as mediator. How would you patch up the quarrel? Remember that in dreams there is no remedy that is beyond reach. Allow such insights to be absorbed into your consciousness – to stretch the imagination is to move closer to reconciliation.

EXERCISE 20

The Shared House of Dreams

We may be able to defuse hostilities by imagining the parts of other people's lives that we ordinarily do not see. If we visualize the shared house before sleep, it may enter our dreams, unconsciously reinforcing the message that all people warrant basic respect and understanding, however much they differ from us in their personality, attitudes, or opinions.

1. Visualize a large house that you live in — the rooms you use and your bedroom are stamped with your personality, but you also have spare rooms for lodgers and guests.

2. Imagine sharing this house with someone with whom you have had an unresolved quarrel. They have their own room but they also make use of the communal facilities.

3. What would a typical day be like? Imagine things they might do that would bother you — perhaps being untidy in the kitchen, or using a pungent brand of perfume or aftershave.

4. Then imagine the neutral things they might do, or the things you might share, such as discussing the late news on TV, or tidying the garden together (imagine holding the garbage sack open for weeds), and so on.

5. In this way, build up a composite picture of their life, and meditate upon it, giving it value in your mind — despite the things that annoy you. It is possible that your imaginative portrait of this person's life in your own house will seep into the imagery of your dreams, and stimulate dreams that will cast illuminating light on the difficulties you have with them.

The Relationship Oracle

*T*hroughout this book we have emphasized that our dream emotions, much more than the actions or settings of our dreams, are the keys that unlock the messages of our unconscious. However, physical symbols do have a major place in interpretation — and our dream emotions give us the mood or atmosphere by which we can more accurately evaluate a dream's symbolism.

The Relationship Oracle provides an alphabetical directory of some of the key relationship symbols with which our dreams may present us. The brief definitions are intended to set the stage for you to personalize each symbol's meaning, and expand it, if necessary, in light of your own life. A series of questions related to each image's appearance in a dream, and how that might reflect on your real-life relationships, will help you to cue your interpretations. Ultimately, a symbol can mean something quite different for one person than it does for another, depending upon personal circumstances and the dream's emotional atmosphere. Try to be open-minded about the Oracle's suggestions: question them with the aim of drawing out further meanings. Soon, the unique language of your unconscious will begin to speak with clarity and eloquence.

The Relationship Oracle

Abandonment *Loss, disappointment. Were you the abandoned or the abandoner? Has someone close recently let you down and, if so, who? Were you badly let down by a parent in your childhood? Do you feel that you have not been fully committed to your current relationship?*

Actor *Self-consciousness. Perhaps you are prone to focusing too much on outward appearances (your own or your partner's), or you are too concerned about your partner's views when you make decisions about yourself. Do you feel that you are under close scrutiny from someone close? Have you been judgmental of someone (with or without their knowledge)? Are you and your partner competitive?*

Alien *Isolation, disconnectedness. Are you confronting an unfamiliar aspect of your relationship? Have you or your partner changed direction recently – perhaps on an issue or in your career? Are major decisions looming, such as moving house or beginning a family?*

Armor *Defensiveness. Could you be shielding your true feelings from someone close? Do you feel particularly insecure about a certain aspect of your relationship? Are you feeling pushed down an avenue you would rather not take — perhaps at work rather than at home?*

Aura *Insight, understanding; or protection. How might your partner or closest friend need your help? What unresolved issues in your relationship require one or other of you to be more perceptive? Do you feel safe in your most important relationship?*

Bell *Unconscious messages; warning of impending argument. Were the bells hand bells or church bells? What things do you know deep down to be true but have brushed aside in waking life? What concerns have you and your partner discussed, but perhaps left unresolved?*

Boat *The course of a relationship. In your dream, was the boat cruising gently or being tossed about by waves? Do you feel that your relationship is steering the right course or headed for turbulent waters? Do you feel in control of the relationship?*

Body *Supportiveness and inner strength. In your dream, were the images of the body strong or weak? In life, do you feel that you have a healthy network of support in your friends? How supportive are you of your partner, and he or she of you? How do you express your support?*

Bridge *Friendship. In your dream, did you cross the bridge, or were you stranded on one side? Was the bridge robust or flimsy? Are there friendships which you feel need attention? What steps could you take to cultivate these relationships? Do you have any anxieties about your ability to make friends?*

Building *You, your partner, or the relationship. The entire edifice might signify the relationship while each room is one of its many facets. What kind of building was in your dream? How might its architecture reflect your relationship? For example, a warehouse may represent holding on to old attitudes, or a castle may suggest hopes and aspirations.*

Bull *Sexuality, sexual competitiveness or temptation; stubbornness. How did the bull appear in your dream — calmly grazing, or ready to charge? How might its actions (or inactions) reflect the tempo of your sexual relationships? Is it that your partner is unmoved on an issue important to you; or are you being stubborn?*

Chasing *Conflict or escape; elusive goals. Were you the chased or the chaser? Were you chasing a person or something intangible? What difficulties are you facing — at work, at home, or among your friends?*

Cleaning *Emotional cleansing. What was being cleaned in your dream? Do you feel the waking need to communicate more openly with your partner? Are there unresolved issues that need your attention?*

Clock *Maturing relationship, sexuality, urgency. Are you aware of time running out in a particular aspect of your relationship? Is someone putting pressure on you to make a decision or get something done? Where would you place your current relationship if it were a stage in life (for example, childhood, teenage years, twenties and so on)?*

Cracks (or breakages) *Change, transforming attitudes; conflict.* How precious to you was the broken item? Was it repaired or swept away? How has your relationship matured over the past months? Has anyone close to you done anything to make you question their friendship? What relationship issues might you be ignoring rather than fixing?

Crown *Superiority, authority, control.* Did you identify with this symbol? Did it feel powerful or authoritative? Was there any sense of helplessness associated with this dream? Do you feel that you control your relationship or that you are controlled? Are there specific (unresolved) issues with figures of authority at work, or in the home?

Death *Transformation (death is rarely meant literally).* Who died in the dream? Did your dream self feel release or anguish at the death? Are you and your partner trying to set aside old differences and move onward? Might there be issues of the relationship's direction to tackle? How do you view its future, and does this coincide with your partner's view?

Dog *Security, loyalty; or attention-seeking, control.* In what ways do you feel vulnerable or unprotected in your relationship? Does the dream-dog's loyalty seem to represent your own or your partner's real-life commitment? Was the dog well-behaved or disobedient?

Father *Strength, authority, protection, problem-solving; dominance, sexual power, aggression.* Whose father appeared in the dream? Did the figure bear any likeness to your own father, or anyone else you know? Was the figure gentle or aggressive? Do you feel that this dream represented your relationship with your family or your partner? If your partner, do you have issues about authority within the relationship?

Festival *Compensation, good news; fear of evaluation, exposure; or being lost in a crowd.* What was the mood of the festival in the dream? Were you reveling among the throng or trying to escape the commotion? Who, known to you, was with you? In real life, are you harnessing any particular secrets for which you fear exposure, perhaps with friends or at work? Do you feel that your voice is unheard within your relationship?

Gift *Desires, needs, friendship.* Did you give or receive the gift in the dream? Who was the giver/recipient if it wasn't you? Was the gift given in kindness? How was it wrapped? In waking life, how do you approach new friendships? Do you feel the need to make an offering in order to put

a relationship back on course? If the giver was known to you, but not a family member or partner, might the person have hidden qualities?

Heart *Nurture, comfort, unconditional love.* In the dream, did the heart appear symbolically, or literally — perhaps as a heart-shaped vase? If literally, what was the item made from? In waking life, do you feel secure in your love for your partner and family, or unsettled? If you have just embarked upon a new relationship, might the heart represent your blossoming feelings for your new partner? Or might it be a warning that you are moving too quickly?

Island *Isolation, misunderstanding; or illicit desire.* Did your dream self feel lonely or relieved to be on an island? Were you trying to reach somewhere else? Was anyone else with you? Is there something that you want to tell your partner but can't find the words to articulate? Do you feel that your partner has left you behind in some way? If the isolation is welcome, are you feeling trapped by your circumstances?

Map *Change, direction, charting a course.* Did you follow the map in your dream? What was it directing you to? If in waking life you have marked out goals within your relationship, could the map be showing you the way toward them? If the map was hard to follow, is one particular goal proving more difficult than you first expected? What changes in direction could benefit your relationship?

Marriage *Certainty, companionship, working together.* Was the marriage your own? If not, whose? Was the bride/groom your partner? Are you and your partner successfully working through difficulties? Have you recently embarked on a common course which previously presented difficulties? How secure do you feel in your relationship?

Maze *Confusion, indecision.* Who was lost in the maze? Were they able to find their way out? Did the person seek help to escape? What could be found at the blind turnings? What was in the center and at the exit? In real life, are you and your partner undecided about something?

Mother *Nurture, spiritual beauty, purity, the giver of life; or aloofness, jealousy, manipulativeness.* Did your dream show your own mother or an archetypal representation? How did she behave toward you? What was she wearing? How did your dream self feel about the figure? How does this compare with how you really feel about your mother?

Mountain *Hope, aspirations; daunting tasks.* How did you feel when you saw the mountain? Were you at the bottom or the top of it, or somewhere in between? Was your partner there with you — by your side or elsewhere on the rockface? If you were at the top or part-way up, what could you see below you? How have you and your partner determined to improve your relationship? Could the mountain, or your positions on it, represent how you might both get on at achieving those aims?

Nudity *Exposure, vulnerability.* Who was naked in your dream? Was it only you among a crowd of clothed people? How did the nudity make you feel? Did you cover yourself up or try to hide? What were the other dream characters' reactions to you? In waking life, have you let slip something you would rather have kept hidden, perhaps from a work colleague or your partner? How might this indiscretion impact on your relationships with people concerned? Do you feel vulnerable to forces beyond your control within a relationship? What insecurities are you harboring?

Police *Authority, justice, fear of punishment; guilt, inferiority.* What role did the police play in your dream? Were they threatening or helpful? What might this authority-figure be asking you to evaluate in your waking life? Have you behaved unfairly recently or is someone behaving unfairly toward you?

Purse (or wallet) *If empty, fear of loss of a loved one or the security offered by a relationship; if full, richness and comfort in a relationship.* What color was the purse or wallet? What was inside it other than money? If it was empty, what did your dream self expect to find in it? Do you feel in waking life that you have recently lost a friend? Has a relationship gone out of kilter or been lacking in some way?

Rainbow *Good news, promise, forgiveness.* Were the colors of the rainbow as they should be (red, orange, yellow, green, blue, indigo, violet)? What waking emotions could each color of your dream rainbow represent? What was the scene on the ground beneath the rainbow? What color was the sky around the rainbow? Are you experiencing any difficulties in any of your relationships? Have you been unforgiving in some way? If the rainbow represents good news, what news might that be?

Storm *Transition; or anger, discord.* Were you alone in the dream when the storm broke? If not, who was with you? Were you inside or outside? Did you get wet? Did the storm make your dream self feel invigorated or scared? In real life are you and your partner going through difficult times or any changes? Are you harboring unexpressed anger against any of your friends or colleagues? How might your dream show you ways to express yourself reasonably?

Teeth *The home; fear of losing a loved one.* How were teeth represented in your dream? Was it your own teeth that were loose or broken? Or did you find them in a jar or other receptacle? Was there a dentist involved? Are you feeling insecure in your most cherished relationships? Are you concerned about the health or happiness of a loved one?

Travel *Change, growing up; or exploration.* Did your dream emotions feel genial and optimistic, or disquieted and unhappy? Were you the one traveling or was it someone close to you? What was your/their mode of transport? What changes are taking place in your most important relationships? Are you and your partner facing a crucial decision? Are you expressing clearly your views on any important factors affecting you both at the moment?

Wall *Blocked communication; or desire to maintain individuality; or need for security.* What lies on the other side of the wall? What lies on your side? Is there a way through the barrier, such as a gap or a gate? Could you climb over it if you tried? Were you happy on your side of the wall or was there a sense of frustration? In waking life, how might you communicate more effectively with your partner or others? Is there someone whom you feel is not listening to you? Do you feel the need to be alone for a while with your thoughts?

Watch *The human heart. If stopped, emotional calmness and quiet; if racing too fast, emotional discord.* Who was wearing the watch in your dream? Is this the watch's owner or did it belong to someone else? Was it old or new; digital or analogue? Was it working properly? What time did it say? Might the dream be about you or another person close to you? How does it reflect your or the other person's emotional health?

Wild animals *Passion.* Can you identify the animals that appeared or were they not only wild but imaginary? How did you feel in their presence — fearful or comfortable? What aspects of your character or desires might they represent? Are you, in waking life, suppressing desire for an individual? Are all your sexual needs being met by your partner? How did you feel when you woke up — aroused or ashamed, or neither?

Bibliography

Adler, A. *On the Interpretation of Dreams*,
International Journal of Individual
Psychology, 2, 3-16, 1936

Cooper, J. *Symbolism*,
Aquarian Press, Wellingborough (UK),
1992

Delaney, G. *Sexual Dreams*,
Piatkus Books, London, 1994; and Fawcett
Books, New York, 1994

Fisher, B. *Rebuilding When Your Relationship Ends*,
Impact Books, London, 1995; and Impact
Publishers, San Luis Obispo (US), 1995

Fontana, D. *Teach Yourself to Dream*,
Duncan Baird Publishers, London, 1996;
and Chronicle Books, San Francisco, 1998

Freud, S. *The Interpretation of Dreams*,
Random House, London, 1994; and Basic
Books, New York, 1953

Garfield, P. *Creative Dreaming*,
Simon & Schuster, New York, 1995

Hall, C. *The Meaning of Dreams*,
McGraw-Hill, New York, 1966

Heyneman, N. *DreamScape*,
Simon & Schuster, New York, 1996

Hobson, A. J. *The Dreaming Brain*,
Basic Books, New York, 1988

Jung, C. G. *Psychology of the Unconscious*,
Routledge, London, 1992; and
Dodd, Mead & Co, New York, 1963

Jung, C. G. *Man and His Symbols*,
Picador, London, 1978; and Doubleday,
New York, 1964

Langs, R. L. *The Daydream Workbook*,
Alliance Publishing, Brooklyn (US), 1995

Mann, A. T. *Elements of Reincarnation*,
Element Books, Shaftesbury (UK), 1995

Matthews, B. *The Herder Symbols Dictionary*,
Chiron Publications, Wilmette (US), 1986

Miller, A. *Banished Knowledge*,
Virago Press, London, 1997; and
Doubleday, New York, 1990

Singer, J. & Pope, K. *The Power of Human
Imagination*, Plenum Press, New York, 1978

Van de Castle, R. *Our Dreaming Mind*,
Ballantine Books, New York, 1994

Vaughan, F. E. *Awakening Intuition*,
Doubleday, New York, 1979

Wallace, B. & Fisher, L. *Consciousness and Behavior*,
Allyn & Bacon, New York, 1991

Weiss, B. *Only Love is Real*,
Piatkus Books, London, 1997;
and Warner Books, New York, 1996

Index

Acknowledgments

The publishers would like to thank the following artists for permission to use their work in this book:

Sandie Turchyn

15, 17, 19, 21, 23, 27, 35,
41, 47, 49, 53, 55, 61, 63,
69, 73, 77, 79, 81, 83, 85,
87, 93, 97, 99, 101, 103,
105, 111, 113, 115, 117, 119,
122, 125

Heidi Younger

11, 13, 20, 25, 27, 29, 31, 33,
37, 38, 43, 45, 50, 57, 59, 65,
67, 71, 75, 89, 90, 95, 107,109,
121, 127, 128, 131, 133, 135, 137

Every effort has been made to credit copyright holders correctly. We apologize for any errors, which we will endeavor to rectify in future editions of this book.

Further Information

If you would like further information about anything discussed in this book, please contact:

Dr. Nicholas Heyneman
2043 East Center Street
PO Box 6208
Pocatello
Idaho 83205–6208
e-mail: neh@srv.net